Migrants and Refugees

Other Books of Related Interest

At Issue Series
The Children of Undocumented Immigrants
Should the US Close Its Borders?
What Is the Impact of Emigration?

Current Controversies Series
Illegal Immigration
Immigration

Global Viewpoints Series
Genocide

Opposing Viewpoints Series
Illegal Immigration
Syria
US Foreign Policy
World Peace

GLOBALVIEWPOINTS

| Migrants and Refugees

M. M. Eboch, Book Editor

GREENHAVEN
PUBLISHING

Published in 2018 by Greenhaven Publishing, LLC
353 3rd Avenue, Suite 255, New York, NY 10010

Articles in Greenhaven Publishing anthologies are often edited for length to meet page
requirements. In addition, original titles of these works are changed to clearly present
the main thesis and to explicitly indicate the author's opinion. Every effort is made to
ensure that Greenhaven Publishing accurately reflects the original intent of the authors.
Every effort has been made to trace the owners of the copyrighted material.

Library of Congress Cataloging-in-Publication Data

Names: Eboch, M.M., editor.
Title: Migrants and refugees / edited by M.M. Eboch.
Description: New York : Greenhaven Publishing, 2018. | Series: Global Viewpoints |
  Includes bibliographical references and index. | Audience: Grades 9-12.
Identifiers: LCCN ISBN 9781534501188 (library bound) | ISBN 9781534501164
  (pbk.)
Subjects: LCSH: Emigration and immigration--Juvenile literature. | Immigrants--
Juvenile literature. | Refugees--Juvenile literature.
Classification: LCC JV6035.M547 2018 | DDC 304.8--dc23

Manufactured in the United States of America

Website: http://greenhavenpublishing.com

Contents

Chapter 2: Whose Responsibility Are Migrants and Refugees?

Chapter 3: The Benefits and Dangers of Immigration

Chapter 5: Better Solutions for Addressing Migrant and Refugee Crises

The number of refugees is rising and the amount of time they spend displaced is lengthening, so solutions must plan for the long term.

Foreword

"*The problems of all of humanity can only be solved by all of humanity.*"
—*Swiss author Friedrich Dürrenmatt*

G lobal interdependence has become an undeniable reality. Mass media and technology have increased worldwide access to information and created a society of global citizens. Understanding and navigating this global community is a challenge, requiring a high degree of information literacy and a new level of learning sophistication.

Building on the success of its flagship series, Opposing Viewpoints, Greenhaven Publishing has created the Global Viewpoints series to examine a broad range of current, often controversial topics of worldwide importance from a variety of international perspectives. Providing students and other readers with the information they need to explore global connections and think critically about worldwide implications, each Global Viewpoints volume offers a panoramic view of a topic of widespread significance.

Drugs, famine, immigration—a broad, international treatment is essential to do justice to social, environmental, health, and political issues such as these. Junior high, high school, and early college students, as well as general readers, can all use Global Viewpoints anthologies to discern the complexities relating to each issue. Readers will be able to examine unique national perspectives while, at the same time, appreciating the interconnectedness that global priorities bring to all nations and cultures.

Material in each volume is selected from a diverse range of sources, including journals, magazines, newspapers, nonfiction books, speeches, government documents, pamphlets, organization newsletters, and position papers. Global Viewpoints is truly global, with material drawn from both international sources available in English and U.S. sources with extensive international coverage.

Features of each volume in the Global Viewpoints series include:

- An **annotated table of contents** that provides a brief summary of each essay in the volume, including the name of the country or area covered in the essay.

- An **introduction** specific to the volume topic.

- A **world map** to help readers locate the countries or areas covered in the essays.

- For each viewpoint, an **introduction** that contains notes about the author and source of the viewpoint explains why material from the specific country is being presented, summarizes the main points of the viewpoint, and offers three **guided reading questions** to aid in understanding and comprehension.

- **For further discussion** questions that promote critical thinking by asking the reader to compare and contrast aspects of the viewpoints or draw conclusions about perspectives and arguments.

- A worldwide list of **organizations to contact** for readers seeking additional information.

- A **periodical bibliography** for each chapter and a **bibliography of books** on the volume topic to aid in further research.

- A comprehensive **subject index** to offer access to people, places, events, and subjects cited in the text, with the countries covered in the viewpoints high- lighted.

Global Viewpoints is designed for a broad spectrum of readers who want to learn more about current events, history, political science, government, international relations, economics, environmental science, world cultures, and sociology— students doing research for class assignments or debates, teachers and faculty seeking to supplement course materials, and others wanting to understand current issues better. By presenting how people in various countries perceive the root causes, current consequences, and proposed solutions to worldwide challenges, Global Viewpoints volumes offer readers opportunities to enhance their global awareness and their knowledge of cultures worldwide.

Introduction

> *"The mass movement of people in
> our world today calls us to reflect
> carefully on the relative weights of
> the obligations and rights that arise
> from our common humanity and
> from our distinctive identities."*
> *—Jesuit priest and human rights
> advocate David Hollenbach*

Immigration is one of the major issues of our time. The number of international migrants has been growing, with 244 million people living in a country other than where they were born in 2015, according to the United Nations. Of those, almost 20 million were refugees, the highest number since World War II. In particular, countries close to Syria have seen rapid increases in refugees since 2012, as Syrians try to escape violent conflict. Some neighboring countries are hosting over 1 million Syrian refugees.

The Merriam-Webster dictionary defines an immigrant as a person who comes to a country to take up permanent residence. The term suggests a person who moves by choice, possibly motivated by the desire to make more money and have a more comfortable lifestyle. A refugee, on the other hand, is a person who flees to a new country in order to escape danger or persecution in their home country. Refugees include men, women, and children, in families or traveling alone.

The term refugee also has an international legal definition. The 1951 Convention relating to the Status of Refugees defines a refugee as someone outside the country of their nationality, who is unable or unwilling to return to that country due to a well-founded fear of being persecuted. Possible reasons for persecution are listed: race, religion, nationality, membership of a particular social group or political opinion. The Convention, along with the Universal Declaration of Human Rights, establishes the rights afforded to people who have been granted refugee status. People facing persecution at home are guaranteed the right to seek and receive asylum in other countries. Additional treaties and updates further modify the definition of a refugee and the legal guidelines surrounding them.

Still, despite these international agreements, each country is allowed to develop its own policies in determining whether someone is a refugee. This can lead to arguments over whether people are truly refugees fleeing persecution, or whether they are immigrants seeking financial gain. Some argue that Syrians are fleeing war, not persecution based on some characteristic they hold, and are therefore not true refugees. This issue is further complicated by environmental disaster. People fleeing drought or flooding may be in danger of death, but not persecution. Do people have a right to escape war and natural disasters, or even poverty, or must they face persecution? This confusion and difference of opinion can lead to refugees being stranded at borders, waiting years for their status to be determined, or being sent back to the country they were trying to escape.

Furthermore, the process to determine refugee status can take years. During that time, refugees may be confined to camps and not allowed to work. This places a burden on the host countries or agencies financing the camp, while the refugees are unable to contribute to society or improve their lives. In other cases, refugees and immigrants may be allowed to live and work in cities and eventually become citizens.

Horror stories about the abuse and deaths of refugees trying to reach safety elicit international outrage. Women and children in particular may face continuing violence and hardship as they flee to a new country, and after they arrive. Still, politicians and citizens argue about how many people should be admitted to their country, and under what restrictions. Some experts argue that rich countries should accept more refugees, or that Christianity demands the welcome of refugees, or that the United States has a responsibility to take in refugees from the Middle East because the US played a role in creating those refugees. Yet others argue that national security comes first and fear that terrorists or drug traffickers may sneak in as refugees. Finally, people debate about the effect immigrants will have on the economy. Statistics show that immigrants often benefit the host country's economy, although large numbers of immigrants can cause an increase in unemployment and a lowering of wages.

Debates rage about how refugees should be treated. Should they be contained in camps, perhaps for years or decades? Should they be given temporary refuge and returned to their home countries as soon as possible? Should they be integrated into society? If so, how is that best accomplished?

Perceptions about and responses to immigration and refugees vary around the world. Different countries have come up with different answers, but few solutions have been completely successful. Ultimately, each country needs to find solutions that work for their unique situation, while cooperating globally to handle the crisis. Global Viewpoints: Migrants and Refugees explores these issues through viewpoints from experts around the world.

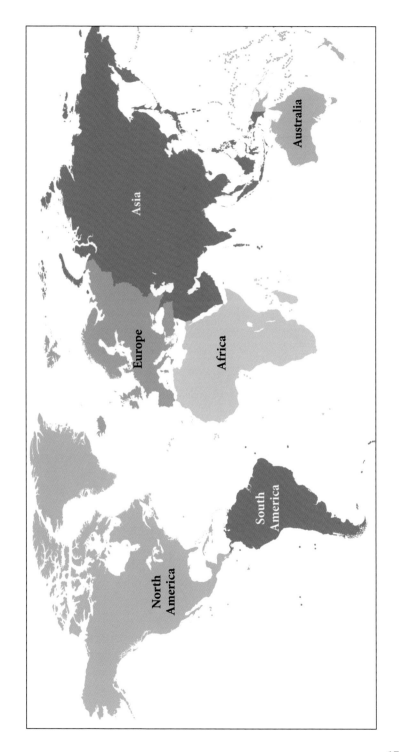

Migrants and Refugees Around the World

Where Migrants Are Moving and Why

United Nations

In the following viewpoint, an excerpt of report from the United Nations provides a detailed look at what countries migrants are leaving and where they are going. This gives a picture of how the world is changing due to migration. The report explores some of the benefits and challenges to international migration. It treats migration as inevitable and often positive. It also suggests that international cooperation is necessary in order to protect human rights. The United Nations Population Division studies population and development, producing updated demographic estimates and projections for all countries.

As you read, consider the following questions:

1. Which two regions have been experiencing the fastest growth in migration?
2. Do migrants usually travel to far distant countries or stay within their own region?
3. Which country hosts the largest number of immigrants?

Introduction

In today's increasingly interconnected world, international migration has become a reality that touches nearly all corners of the globe, often making distinctions between countries of origin, transit and destination obsolete. Modern transportation has made it easier, cheaper and faster for people to move. At the same time conflict, poverty, inequality and lack of decent jobs are among the reasons that compel people to leave their homes in search of better futures for themselves and their families.

When supported by appropriate policies, migration can contribute to inclusive and sustainable economic growth and development in both home and host communities. In 2014, migrants from developing countries sent home an estimated US $436 billion in remittances; a 4.4 percent increase over the 2013 level (World Bank 2015), far exceeding official development assistance and, excluding China, foreign direct investment. These funds are often used to improve the livelihoods of families and communities through investments in education, health, sanitation, housing and infrastructure. Countries of destination can also benefit from migration. In countries of destination, migrants often fill critical labour shortages, create jobs as entrepreneurs, and contribute in terms of taxes and social security contributions. Migrants, as some of the most dynamic members of society, can also forge new paths in science, medicine and technology and enrich their host communities by promoting cultural diversity.

In spite of the many benefits of migration, migrants themselves remain among the most vulnerable members of society. They are often the first to lose their job in the event of an economic downturn, often working for less pay, for longer hours, and in worse conditions than national workers. While for many migration is an empowering experience, others endure human rights violations, abuse and discrimination. Migrants, particularly women and children, are too often victims of human trafficking and the heinous forms of exploitation that human trafficking entails. Further, in many parts of the world, migration remains one of the few options for people, particularly young people, to find decent work, and escape poverty, persecution and violence.

The 2030 Agenda for Sustainable Development recognises the positive contribution of migrants for inclusive growth and sustainable development. It further recognises that international migration is a multi-dimensional reality of major relevance for the development of countries of origin, transit and destination, which requires coherent and comprehensive responses. International cooperation is critical to ensure safe, orderly and regular migration involving full respect for human rights and the humane treatment of migrants and refugees.

[...]

The pace of growth in the migrant stock varies across major areas. Asia and Oceania experienced the fastest average annual growth rate in the migrant stock. Between 2000 and 2015, the number of international migrants in Asia and Oceania grew by an average of 2.8 per cent per year. Latin America and the Caribbean recorded the third fastest average annual growth rate in the international migrant stock during this period (2.3 per cent), followed by Africa (2.2 per cent). Europe and Northern America, where the size of the migrant stock was already large, experienced a slightly slower pace of change, with an average annual growth rate of 2 per cent for each.

Most of the world's migrants live in a handful of countries. In 2015, 67 per cent of all international migrants in the world were living in just twenty countries. The largest number of international migrants resided in the United States of America: 47 million, equal to 19 per cent of the world's total. Germany and the Russian Federation hosted the second and third largest numbers of migrants worldwide (around 12 million each), followed by Saudi Arabia (10 million), the United Kingdom of Great Britain and Northern Ireland (nearly 9 million), and the United Arab Emirates (8 million). Of the top twenty destinations of international migrants worldwide, nine were in Asia, seven in Europe, two in Northern America, and one each in Africa and Oceania.

Trends in the stock of international migrants differ widely by country. Between 2000 and 2015, the number of migrants grew in 167 countries or areas worldwide. In 63 of these, including France, Germany and the United States of America, the international migrant stock grew by less than 2 per cent per annum. In 104 countries or areas, however, the pace of growth during the period 2000-2015 was considerably faster, with 19 countries or areas recording an average annual growth rate of 6 per cent or more. Among the countries or areas with the most pronounced growth during this period were Italy, Spain, Thailand and the United Arab Emirates. In contrast, in 61 countries or areas, the stock of international migrants declined during the period 2000-2015. In 39 countries or areas, including India, the Islamic Republic of Iran, the Russian Federation and Ukraine, the pace of decline was less than 2 per cent per annum. In 22 countries or areas, however, the international migrant stock shrunk more rapidly, with 10 countries or areas recording an average decline of more than 4 per cent per annum.

The number of refugees worldwide has reached the highest level since World War II. In 2014, the total number of refugees in the world was estimated at 19.5 million, representing about 8 per cent of all international migrants (United Nations High Commissioner for Refugees 2015). Developing regions hosted 86 per cent of the world's refugees (12.4 million persons), the highest value in more than two decades. The least developed countries provided asylum to 3.6 million refugees, or 25 per cent of the global total. In 2014, Turkey became the largest refugee-hosting country worldwide, with 1.6 million refugees. Turkey was followed by Pakistan (1.5 million), Lebanon (1.2 million), the Islamic Republic of Iran (1.0 million), Ethiopia and Jordan (0.7 million each). More than half (53 per cent) of refugees under UNHCR's mandate come from just three countries: the Syrian Arab Republic (3.9 million), Afghanistan (2.6 million) and Somalia (1.1 million).

[…]

In many parts of the globe, migration occurs primarily between countries that are located within the same major area of the world. The majority of the international migrants originating from Asia (60 per cent, or 62 million persons), Europe (66 per cent, or 40 million), Oceania (59 per cent, or 1 million) and Africa (52 per cent, or 18 million) live in another country of their major area of origin. In contrast, the majority of international migrants born in Latin America and the Caribbean (84 per cent, or 32 million) and Northern America (73 per cent, or 3 million) reside in a country outside their major area of birth.

Migration between countries that are located within the same major area is increasing. Between 2000 and 2015, the share of international migrants who remained within their own major area of birth increased in Asia, Europe, Latin America and the Caribbean, and Oceania. Conversely, for migrants born in Africa and Northern America, the proportion of those living in a country outside of their major area of birth increased. For Africa this has been accompanied by an increase in the share of African foreign-born persons living in Asia, Europe, Northern America and Oceania, while for Northern America it resulted in an increase in the share of persons living in Asia, Latin America and the Caribbean, and Oceania.

Asia is the origin with the largest number of persons who are living outside their major area of birth. In 2015, there were 42 million international migrants born in Asia but living elsewhere. Of these, the majority were living in Europe (20 million), followed by Northern America (17 million) and Oceania (3 million). Migrants born in Latin America and the Caribbean represented the second largest diaspora group with 32 million persons living outside their major area of birth. The majority of these migrants were living in Northern America (26 million) and Europe (5 million). Europe had the third largest number of persons living outside their major area of birth (22 million). These migrants were primarily residing in Asia and Northern America (8 million each) and Oceania (3 million).

Between 2000 and 2015, some regional "corridors" grew very rapidly. Asia was one of the fastest growing destinations for migrants from Africa, with an annual average growth rate of 4.2 per cent, equal to an absolute increase of nearly 2 million migrants during this period. For foreign-born persons from Asia, the fastest growing corridors outside of Asia were from Asia to Oceania (4.8 per cent increase per annum, yielding 2 million more migrants during the period 2000-2015) and from Asia to Northern America (2.7 per cent per annum, yielding 6 million more). One of the fastest-growing destinations for migrants originating from Latin America and the Caribbean was Europe (6.4 per cent per annum, or 3 million more). For foreign-born persons coming from Europe, one of the fastest-growing destinations was Africa (3.2 per cent per annum, or 0.5 million more), whereas for foreign-born originating from Northern America, it was Latin America and the Caribbean (3.4 per cent per annum, or 0.5 million more).

India now has the largest "diaspora" in the world, followed by Mexico, the Russian Federation and China. In 2015, 16 million persons from India were living outside of their country of birth compared to 12 million from Mexico. Other countries with large diasporas included the Russian Federation (11 million), China (10 million), Bangladesh (7 million), and Pakistan and Ukraine (6 million each). Of the top twenty countries or areas of origin of international migrants, 11 were in Asia, 6 in Europe, and 1 each in Africa, Latin America and the Caribbean, and Northern America.

Between 2000 and 2015, some countries have experienced a rapid growth in the size of their diaspora populations. Among the countries and areas with the fastest average annual growth rate during this period were the Syrian Arab Republic (13.1 per cent per annum), Romania (7.3 per cent per annum), Poland (5.1 per cent per annum) and India (4.5 per cent per annum). In Syria much of this increase was due to the large outflow of refugees and asylum seekers following the conflict in the area.

"Diasporas" from some countries of origin tend to concentrate in particular countries of destination. Mexico's diaspora is concentrated in just one country: the United States of America. In 2015, the United States of America hosted some 12 million persons born in Mexico, equal to nearly 98 per cent of all Mexicans living abroad. Other examples of countries with diaspora populations settled predominantly in one country include Algeria (in France), Burkina Faso (in Côte d'Ivoire), Cuba and El Salvador (in the United States of America), and New Zealand (in Australia). In contrast, India's diaspora is more evenly spread out between a number of destination countries, including the United Arab Emirates (3 million), and Pakistan and the United States of America (2 million each). Several countries of the former Soviet Union, including the Russian Federation and Ukraine, also have more evenly distributed diaspora populations.

The contribution of international migration to population dynamics

The number of international migrants worldwide has grown faster than the world's population. As a result of this faster growth rate, the share of migrants in the total population reached 3.3 per cent in 2015, up from 2.8 in 2000. There were, however considerable differences between major areas. In Europe, Northern America and Oceania, international migrants accounted for at least 10 per cent of the population. By contrast, in Africa, Asia, and Latin America and the Caribbean, less than 2 per cent of the population consisted of international migrants. International migration contributes significantly to population growth in many parts of the world, and reverses negative growth in some countries or areas. Between 2000 and 2015, positive net migration[2] contributed to 42 per cent of the population growth in Northern America and 32 per cent in Oceania. In Europe, the size of the population would have declined during the period 2000-2015 in the absence of positive net migration, whereas in Africa, Asia, and Latin America and the Caribbean, negative net migration contributed marginally to slowing the pace of population growth. The impact of negative net migration is generally modest for countries with large populations.

Migrants and Refugees

Home to 1.6 million refugees, Turkey has hosted the largest number of immigrants so far this century. Lebanon and Jordan have also risen up the rankings, as the chart below shows, as the current human rights crisis unfolds in Syria.

While other countries, such as the United States and Canada, have remained relatively consistent since the year 2000, nations located close to Syria have seen a rapid increase in refugees since 2012.

At the end of 2014, there were 19.5 million refugees in the world and a total of 59.5 million people forcibly displaced as a result of persecution, conflict, generalized violence, or human rights violations. That is the equivalent of 42,500 people every day. If you were to create a country made of all those displaced people, it would be the 24th largest country in the world.

In the past year or so, most refugees have been coming from Syria; in 2014 it was Afghanistan. Contrary to Western criticism that the Middle East is not doing enough, 95% of all Syrian refugees are now hosted in neighbouring countries. Turkey has welcomed 1.59 million refugees while Lebanon brought in 1.15 million. Iran has 982,000.

While the Syrian crisis dominates headlines, the volume of refugees flowing out of Afghanistan and Somalia is no less troubling. Pakistan hosted the second-largest number of refugees last year due to the 2.59 million Afghans seeking refuge. Meanwhile, 1.11 million Somalians were forced to flee home, many relocating to Ethiopia.

Over half of all refugees are children under the age of 18.

"Which country has hosted the most refugees?" by Donald Armbrecht, World Economic Forum, December 17, 2015. https://www.weforum.org/agenda/2015/12/which-country-has-hosted-the-most-refugees-this-century. Licensed under CC BY 4.0.

During the period 2000-2015, for instance, negative net migration had a relatively small impact on population change in countries or areas with large populations, including Bangladesh, China, India and Mexico. However, for smaller countries or areas, including the Small Island Developing States (SIDS), the impact can be more substantial. In the Federated States of Micronesia and the Marshall

Islands, for example, whereas the size of the population declined during the period 2000-2015 owing to negative net migration, it would have increased under a scenario of zero-net migration.

Net migration is projected to have a significant impact on the future size of populations in a number of major areas. In Europe, while current trends in migration will not be enough to compensate for the surplus of deaths over births, this decline would have been even more pronounced, and started earlier, under a zero-net-migration scenario. Likewise, in Northern America the size of the population would start to decline in 2040 under a zero-net-migration scenario, while in Oceania the decline in total population would be two times larger by 2050.

Migration can contribute to reducing slowing the long-term trend towards population aging. Because international migrants tend to comprise larger proportions of working-age persons compared to the overall population, positive net migration can contribute to reducing old-age dependency ratios. In many parts of the world, the old-age dependency ratio would be even higher in the absence of net migration. Assuming zero net migration, the old-age dependency ratio of Europe in 2050 would rise to 51 persons age 65 or over per 100 persons of working age, compared to 48 per 100 assuming a continuation of current migration patterns. For Northern America and Oceania, the old age dependency ratio would rise to 43 and 34 per 100, respectively, with zero-net migration, compared to 38 and 30 per 100 if current levels of migration continue.

While international migration can play a role in modifying dependency ratios, it cannot reverse the trend of population aging. Even assuming a continuation of current migration patterns, all major areas of the world are projected to have significantly higher old-age dependency ratios in 2050.[3] In Asia, for every 100 persons of working age, there will be 28 dependent older persons in 2050 compared to 11 dependent older persons in 2015. Likewise, during the period 2015-2050, old-age dependency ratios are projected to increase from 26 to 48 per 100 in Europe, from

22 to 38 per 100 in Northern America, from 11 to 31 per 100 in Latin America and the Caribbean, and from 18 to 30 per 100 in Oceania. Only Africa is projected to have an old-age dependency ratio below 10 persons aged 65 or over per 100 persons of working age in 2050.

Ratification of legal instruments related to international migration

The United Nations has five legal instruments related to international migration. These are: (a) the 1951 Convention relating to the Status of Refugees, (b) the 1967 Protocol Relating to the Status of Refugees, (c) the 1990 International Convention on the Protection of the Rights of All Migrants and Members of Their Families, (d) the 2000 Protocol to Prevent, Suppress and Punish Trafficking in Persons, Especially Women and Children, and (e) the 2000 Protocol against the Smuggling of Migrants by Land, Sea and Air. Together with the instruments on the rights of migrant workers adopted by the International Labour Organization (ILO), these form the basis of the international normative and legal framework on international migration.

The ratification of the United Nations legal instruments related to international migrants and migration remains uneven. The 1951 Refugee Convention and its 1967 Protocol have been ratified by 145 and 146 United Nations Member States, respectively. Likewise, two thirds of countries have ratified the two protocols seeking to stem irregular migration in the form of human trafficking and migrant smuggling. However, only one quarter of countries have ratified the 1990 International Convention on the Protection of the Rights of All Migrants and Members of Their Families. As of October 2015, 36 Member States had ratified all five of the United Nations legal instruments related to international migration, while 14 Member States had ratified none of the relevant instruments.

Endnotes

2. Net international migration refers to the difference between the number of immigrants and the number of emigrants. If more people immigrate to a country than emigrate from it, the latter gains population from positive net migration. When more people emigrate than immigrate, the country loses population through negative net migration.

3. The old-age dependency ratio is a commonly used measure of the potential need for social and economic support in a population. It is calculated by dividing the population aged 65 years or older by the working-age population, aged 15 to 64 years old. In general, a higher value of this ratio indicates that each potential worker needs to support a larger number of potentially dependent persons aged 65 years or older.

A Hard Life for Refugee Families

Kelly Montgomery

In the following viewpoint, Kelly Montgomery of Mercy Corps describes some of the hazards facing refugees from war-torn countries. She shares a glimpse of life for refugees in transit, suggesting it is difficult and exhausting. Montgomery also describes life for the people who help refugees as arduous. Kelly Montgomery is a digital content producer at Mercy Corps, an organization that provides humanitarian and development assistance around the world.

As you read, consider the following questions:

1. How many refugees arrived in Europe in 2015?
2. What services do humanitarian organizations provide to refugees?
3. What does Mercy Corps suggest must happen in order to ultimately solve the problems refugees face?

Right now, close to 12,000 refugees are crowded at Greece's border with Macedonia, waiting and hoping to be allowed safe passage as they flee towards the safety and promise of northern Europe.

Recently, the route north through the Balkans was officially closed — and now, refugees who flee across the sea risk being sent back as soon as they arrive. And so families already trapped in

"Refugee Families Face Uncertainty in Europe," by Kelly Montgomery, Mercy Corps, March 28, 2016. Reprinted by permission.

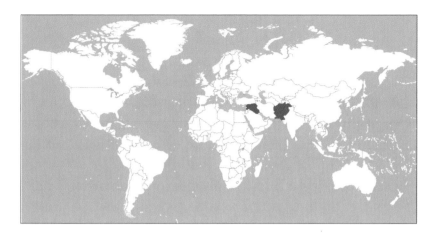

Greece wait, with children strapped to their backs and carrying few belongings, for a second chance at a more peaceful future.

Our team worked tirelessly all winter in Greece, Serbia and Macedonia to help refugee families keep moving forward—offering food, temporary shelter, winter supplies and critical information.

But now, the excitement and relief refugees felt in the fall has been replaced with uncertainty.

Refugee arrivals on the shores of Greece peaked last summer, when approximately 10,000 refugees—from Syria, Iraq, Afghanistan, Pakistan, and as far as Eritrea—were making the dangerous journey across the Mediterranean Sea and into Europe every day.

More than 1 million refugees arrived to Europe by sea in 2015. Another 144,000 have already arrived in 2016.

Facing uncertainty and a journey through cold and potentially snowy conditions, fewer refugees are making the trip—but they are still coming—with some 2,500 arriving on Greece's islands, exhausted and weary, every day.

Many refugees feel that they have no choice. After five years of war in Syria, and pockets of conflict and violence in nearby Iraq and Afghanistan, there is little hope for a family trying to survive or a mother caring for her young children.

So each day, families board tiny rubber boats, crowded with dozens of other refugees — most wearing counterfeit life jackets — and hope that they make it across alive.

The refugee route: A grueling journey

While the trip across the sea is daunting and dangerous, it was just the beginning for refugees who were trying to make it all the way to Germany or Scandinavia. After taking a ferry to Greece's mainland, refugees had to pass through Macedonia, Serbia, Croatia, Slovenia or Hungary, and Austria before they reach Germany, where many refugees hope to stay and build a new life.

Most of this grueling journey was spent on the move — boarding trains in the middle of the night, crowding onto buses, and walking across rough terrain just to get to the next stop. There's little time for rest. Refugee families only spent a matter of hours, or a day or two at most, passing through countries like Macedonia and Serbia. And the conditions were often treacherous.

At the border between Macedonia and Serbia, refugees had to walk approximately one and a half miles across a barren field, carrying whatever they brought with them. Because it's a border crossing, organizations like Mercy Corps were only allowed to help people on either side. Refugees had to make the walk in between by themselves.

Late last year, the field was pounded by heavy rains, and the path turned to knee-deep mud. Come January, the mud froze and was covered by a layer of snow. The winter weather here takes no mercy on those passing through.

Mercy Corps has been working along the refugee route from Greece to Croatia since last fall, helping people continue forward on their journey as safely as possible. In Macedonia and Serbia, it was a skeleton team. Once only three dedicated staff, the team grew to a small but mighty group of seven.

Near the border, on either side, staff offered information, translation services, and assistance with transportation, particularly for the disabled or elderly. Signage in the area is sparse, and not often translated into Arabic or other languages. Family members were sometimes separated, and our team worked to reunite them as quickly as possible.

To help stave off exhaustion and the brutal winter temperatures, we also ran temporary shelters that offered heaters and safe spaces for families to rest before they continued on towards northern Europe.

"There is no life in Iraq and Syria ..."

The trip was difficult enough for most, but it seemed impossible at times for pregnant women with small children, the elderly and people with disabilities.

Khalid, 55, is originally from Baghdad and needs a wheelchair to get around. When the war in Iraq erupted years ago, he and his family fled to Syria. But the violence in Syria was too much to bear, so Khalid and his son became refugees for a second time as they escaped Syria to make the journey towards Europe.

"We left Syria because of the war. There is no life in Iraq and Syria so we have to go somewhere else," said Khalid.

He was supposed to receive assistance so that his whole family could leave Syria, but the help never came.

Without enough money to bring his wife, Khalid and his son began the long trip, hoping that she'll be able to join them eventually. "We hope one day we will send money to her in Syria to bring her to Germany," he said.

When Khalid and his son arrived by train to Tabanovce, Macedonia, they took some time to warm up and rest in a Mercy Corps shelter before our team helped transport them by van to the Serbian border. It was a difficult trip for Khalid, but it's the best choice he feels he can make for his family.

"The road to here was honestly a difficult part. The path to here was tiring. Very tiring," said Khalid. "It's hard traveling in a wheelchair because roads aren't made to accommodate a wheelchair — they're all rock or dirt. The road kept shaking under my chair, it was harder to be in the chair than to walk."

But Khalid perseveres — he knows that if they can make it to Germany, his son, who also has a disability, will have hope for a better life and a stronger future.

"My son needs a major surgery. He was born with a defect. He can't see with his right eye, and can't breathe on the right side," said Khalid. "We're hoping he can have this surgery in Germany. There aren't any doctors who can help in Syria."

A small, but mighty team helps refugees

Our staff members in Macedonia and Serbia worked day and night all winter to help refugees like Khalid continue forward. One of those dedicated team members is Kusang Tamang, who left his position in Nepal for a few months to join the effort in the Balkans.

In an emergency situation like the refugee crisis, things can get hectic. "When I first came here I was doing everything, and we didn't have shifts," Tamang said. "I would be working in the morning and at night. It could be on the Macedonian side or on the Serbian side of the border."

Refugee trains arrived at all hours of the day, and through the night, so the team had to create shifts to make sure that they could help at any time. The normal shift was from 5 p.m. to 1 a.m., when the team determined there was the most need for assistance.

"But if there is a need, a lot of people coming through, we will work until 3:30 a.m.," said Tamang. "There was one time when one of our officers worked until 5:30 in the morning."

The team had one van on the Macedonian side of the border, and two on the Serbian side. They looked out for the most vulnerable individuals and offered help with transportation to the refugee processing centers, or to a temporary shelter for rest. "With one van the average is about 80 people that we transport in one shift," Tamang said.

Helping refugees like Khalid gave Tamang and the other team members a sense of purpose. They know how important it is to offer kindness and hope during such a difficult process. "The work is very rewarding," Tamang said. "It feels good at the end of the shift to know that you actually helped people, and to see that you are making a difference."

"What stands out to me is the people saying thank you. Because they have been abused, they have been harassed on their way here, and then when someone helps them, they really appreciate that."

Best solution: Solve the refugee crisis

Since September, our work along the refugee route in Greece, Macedonia and Serbia has reached approximately 80,000 people.

When refugees arrived in Greece this winter, our team there offered food, shelter, information, winter supplies and cash assistance to help them continue their journey. As they moved through the Balkans, Mercy Corps staff helped provide transportation, translation, information, shelter and more winter supplies if refugees needed them.

As refugees pushed on past the Balkans and to more hopeful futures in northern Europe, one thing became clear— despite incredible challenges, refugees will keep coming until the fighting stops.

"The best solution would be to resolve the conflict. I know — it's easy to say, hard to do," said Mercy Corps team member Kamil Qandil.

"Humanitarian assistance is needed, but it's not a solution. We can try to provide dignity and respect and support people, but the solution should be political. We can carry on with humanitarian assistance for as long as it is needed, but it does not resolve the source of the conflict."

Children in Danger Should Not Be Turned Away

Valeria Gomez Palacios

In the following viewpoint, Valeria Gomez Palacios describes the plight of children displaced from Mexico and Central America. She describes some of the violence these children are fleeing and claims that returning them to their country of origin would be the same as granting them a death sentence. In her view, this makes the situation a refugee crisis rather than an issue of immigration. She believes governments should be more receptive to child refugees. Valeria Gomez Palacios is a freelance writer and research specialist.

As you read, consider the following questions:

1. How many children were forcibly displaced from Mexico and Central America during the year cited?
2. What is the difference between an immigrant and a refugee?
3. What is the principle of non refoulement?

According to the United Nations High Commissioner on Refugees, more than 90,000 children from Mexico and Central America will be forcibly displaced by the end of the year. 90,000 Children. Behind these children are 90,000 individual tragedies. Children being killed and traumatized by gang violence,

"The US Faces a Refugee Crisis, Not an Immigration Problem," by Valeria Gomez Palacios, Foreign Policy Journal, July 25, 2014. First appeared in Foreign Policy Journal. Reprinted by permission of the author.

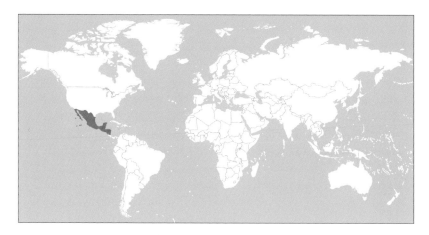

children with broken families, forced to abandon their homes and avail themselves from the protection of another state.

The responsibility of this situation lies in the poor governance of the governments of El Salvador, Honduras, Guatemala and Mexico. These Central American countries have some of the highest murder rates in the world and their governments' inability to subdue the violence has caused this situation to reach its current state. These children are not seeking economic benefit; they are fleeing because the violence and instability in their home country has escalated to the degree that warrants them international protection and the status of asylum seekers. They are escaping due to a well-founded fear of being killed and hurt because their own government cannot provide for their safety and security and thus they must avail themselves from the shelter of another state. The issue has escalated to the point that this is no longer an immigration story but a refugee crisis.

The heart drenching stories behind the refugee crisis range from an 11 year old abandoning Guatemala to help support his bedridden dying mother to a possible 17 year old with a curiosity that could have unravel the world yet statistically he is bound to get sucked into the violence of cartels. In a world in which human beings should enjoy freedom from prosecution, freedom from want and economy security, protecting refugees needs to be proclaimed

What Makes a Refugee?

The president of the Dominican Republic faced a tough question after the 2010 earthquake hit Haiti and left hundreds of thousands of Haitians homeless—should he open his borders to them? There was no international law to guide the president's decision, said Walter Kälin, former Representative of the UN Secretary-General on the Human Rights of Internally Displaced Persons, because the displaced "were not protected as refugees" by international law. There is a gap in international norms.

Mr. Kälin said every year between 12-45 million people are displaced by sudden onset disasters; this number doesn't include those displaced by slow-onset disasters. "Displacement is one of the biggest challenges we are facing right now," he said.

Mr. Kälin described another case where 100,000 people fleeing drought in the Horn of Africa showed up at the border to Kenya, saying they had lost their crops and animals and would die if they weren't allowed in the country.

"And again, the question: are they refugees? How should they be treated? Do they have a right to access neighboring countries?" he asked.

Mr. Kälin said displacement is not just a humanitarian issue, and mitigation should include investing in development. "Development interventions can help to stabilize, to prevent displacement," he said. "And I think that's a big enough issue to be worthwhile to be included in this sustainable development agenda, into the focus areas, the goals and targets. And I very much hope that this will happen."

He said another crucial way to mitigate displacement is to listen to climate change scientists. These scientists model climate and can show areas vulnerable to rising seas, drought, and desertification—places where displacement is likely. "People will move, and it will be increasingly large numbers. We can wait and do nothing. But we also can be prepared, because it's foreseeable," he said.

"What Makes a Refugee? As Impact of Natural Disasters Grows, Definition Leaves Gaps,"
by Jeremie Labbe, International Peace Institute (IPI), April 8, 2014.

as the highest aspiration of the international community and the common people. We need to remind the governments of El

Salvador, Honduras and Mexico that they have a responsibility to these children and many others who might consider fleeing their home country. They have the responsibility to build up their social structure and provide the basic needs, shelter and structure needed for a stable and safe society. Politicians, judges and polices forces can no longer ignore their duty. They have to stop the immunity and the extortion and start protecting. These governments have to ensure that if given a choice children would never abandon their homes… because to these 90,000 children that fled, staying was no longer a choice.

The core concern in this situation should not be a concern with borders but a concern with the life and dignity of these children. Although the responsibility of this inflow of unaccompanied minors clearly lies within their home government this does not mean the governments where these children are seeking refuge should shy away from their responsibilities under international law. The children arriving to the US borders are living a life of terror. They fear for themselves, they worry about the family members they left behind. They are scared of getting trafficked and sucked into the violence. They want to avoid drugs and death. Among these children are girls that do not want to get kidnapped, beaten and raped by gangs. Girls that are seen as sexual objects and threatened if they don't obey. At the tender age of 14 they fear the unknown dangers and uncertainty hunts them. Some of these refugees are orphans, some are teenagers escaping the cross fire and gang violence, others are escaping the vestige of a failed system that could not provide for them; whatever they are fleeing from it is clear that to them staying was no longer a choice.

The 1951 Convention Relating to the Status of Refugees defines a "refugee" as any person who is outside their country of origin and unable or unwilling to return there or to avail themselves of its protection. These children long for a better world, some want to be writers others engineers yet they grew up in a world of violence where their dreams are unattainable and a death a day is considered normality. The principle of non refoulement, considered a norm of customary international law, states that a state may not oblige a person to return to a territory where the person will be exposed to persecution and the violation of its dignity. Returning these children back to their home country would not only expose them to danger but it would be the same as granting them a death sentence. Furthermore the 1966 Bangkok Principles on Status and Treatment of Refugees expands the definition of a refugee to include a person fleeing "external aggression, or events seriously disturbing public order (such as those happening in Central America) in either part or the whole of [their] country of origin' and their lawful dependents." Children have a pure heart, they don't understand politics or immigration laws but they do understand humanity and, despite everything they have endured, they believe that there is still hope in the world for them. They see this hope in the United States, Nicaragua, Costa Rica and Panama and that is why they come here. The convention and the declaration thus grant these children the rights to seek a safe haven and simultaneously oblige the signatory countries to grant them asylum.

The fundamental responsibility to these children is not admitting them here or there or sending them away but to assist them through democratic attachments and constitutional norms. Under the 1951 Convention Relating to the Status of Refugees the states agree to provide assistance to refugees such as administrative assistance, legal identity papers, travel document, and the ability to naturalize as citizens. In regards to basic human rights, article IV of the conventions provides for the "treatment no less favorable than that generally accorded to aliens in similar circumstances, with due regard to basic human rights as recognized in generally accepted international instruments." The 90,000 children are not only in their right to be granted asylum and protection but to be treated with respect and dignity.

What is then the role of the U.S. in this situation? The media attention has been focused on how the United States has responded to the massive influx of refugees at its borders. It is important to remind the United States that rather than being an immigration problem, this is a refugee crisis and thus the United States must respond to the petitions and needs of these children accordingly. The United States is not the only country receiving asylum seekers due to this crisis, Nicaragua, Costa Rica and Panama, countries with smaller resources, have all reported receiving an increase in asylum seekers yet the United States is the only country turning them down.

The United States needs to be reminded that asylum seekers have rights, and ultimately the right to asylum is stipulated under international law as a human right; thus spontaneous acts of humanitarianism will not suffice to define the institutional commitments democracies have to aid these children. In other words, according to international law regarding refugee policy the United States, Nicaragua, Costa Rica and Panama do not only have a moral duty to help these children but an obligation to do so. When a state complies with international agreements it is not a mere act of compassion or humanitarian kindness but rather a duty and a responsibility because above all nationality, humanity comes first and furthermost. If there is a category of asylum seekers that might make states more inclined to abide by international law agreements, then children traveling alone definitely meets this criteria.

The White House has stated that most unaccompanied minors arriving to the border are unlikely to qualify for humanitarian relief and thus will have no legal basis to stay in the country; yet the United States is a signatory to various conventions that specifically reflect the principle of non refoulment, thus, in fact, granting the children a legal basis to stay in the country as asylum seekers. Statements made by Homeland Security stating that the flood of unaccompanied minors crossing the border is a legal and a humanitarian dilemma further back up the status of the children as asylum seekers. Additionally, section 207(b) of the Immigration & Nationality Act, 8 U.S. Code Sec.1157 (b) states that if an unforeseen emergency refugee situation exists, then the admission of certain refugees in response to the emergency refugee situation is justified by grave humanitarian concern. Under this code the president of the United States has the ability to rightfully declare these children as refugees. Failing to grant asylum to these unaccompanied minors would violate this code, and deporting them would be breaking international law and would also violate the Trafficking and Victims Re-authorization Act of 2008, and more importantly the Homeland Security Act of 2002. According to the law of the United States; citizens from a non bordering states most be taken by the Border Patrol and transferred to the Office of Refugee Resettlement, and because most of these children are coming from Honduras and El Salvador, any deportation currently made is deemed illegal. By deporting these children the United States is not only knowingly violation international law but its very own national law as well. In order to settle the humanitarian issues this crisis has brought; respecting international as well as national asylum and refugee laws is necessity.

In the following weeks, when the U.S. decides the fate of these children, it needs to keep in mind that any decision to strengthen the border needs to also include protection from sending children back to places where they might face violence as specified in the international conventions and agreements the United States is a signatory to. The government's policies need to be strengthened to not only encompass immigration reform but also a clear and concise policy in abiding by international asylum law principles. It needs to set up well-established institutional settings and legal procedures that actively abide to asylum law and practices. Asylum officers and judges need to be trained to actively deal with these traumatized children, border patrol agents need to adequately screen children and identify those fleeing persecution, traffickers, and sexual exploitation. They need to be protected and ensured full protection and rights granted to them as asylum seekers, they need to be represented by lawyers and granted the whole spectrum of due process. The United States has a moral duty to ensure that they are protecting these children rather than just handing death sentences. The United States thus needs to abide by the principle of non-refoulment, which forbids the rendering of a victim back to a place where they might be persecuted or where their lives or freedoms could be threatened.

How the United State reacts to the political risks associated with asylum, the management of forced migration and its responsibility, the role of intermediate actors, asylum interviewers, local governments, immigration judges, and security staff will ultimately determine its success in solving the crisis. Ultimately, in order to help consolidate the Central American crisis the United States needs to inspire a doctrine that respect asylum laws and that is consistent with American laws and the values on which the country was founded. The United States is known as a humanitarian nation, a nation with character, the land of the free, founded on taking in the poor, the hungry, the tired, the huddled masses yearning to breathe free. As the symbol of the Unite States stands "a mighty woman with a torch, whose flame is the imprisoned lightning, and her name, Mother of Exiles," now is the time for the United States to lift its lamp besides the golden door.

As for the role of the common people, the majority of us keep humanity in high regard in principle but we have no time to give it a meaning of our own. The refugee crisis in Central America means that over 90,000 lives are being uprooted. These are 90,000 desperate souls trying to find refuge away from home and we have a responsibility to care and be concerned about the actions and policies of our governments regarding other humans. Our focus should be to protect and assist these innocent children caught in the midst of the conflict. Human security pertains above all to the safety and well being of all the people everywhere. Human security is not about states and nations, but about individuals and people. A policy in regards to the crisis in Central America needs to shift away from nationalistic concerns. We need to ensure these refugees are protected and granted basic rights because above all nationality; humanity needs to be our first concern. There is a human face to the US border crisis; these are 90,000 children that, had we not been lucky enough, could have ultimately been our own.

Female Refugees at Risk

Tirana Hassan

In the following viewpoint, Tirana Hassan describes some of the hazards faced specifically by female refugees. They often feel unsafe and face harassment, pressure to have sex, and violence. She suggests that governments must take greater steps to ensure the safety of female refugees. Tirana Hassan is director of Crisis Response at Amnesty International, an international organization focused on human rights.

As you read, consider the following questions:

1. What hazards do refugees face that are primarily problems for women and girls?
2. What percentage of women interviewed felt unsafe during their journeys as refugees?
3. Were police generally helpful in protecting female refugees?

G overnments and aid agencies are failing to provide even basic protections to women refugees traveling from Syria and Iraq. New research conducted by Amnesty International shows that women and girl refugees face violence, assault, exploitation and sexual harassment at every stage of their journey, including on European soil.

"Female refugees face physical assault, exploitation and sexual harassment on their journey through Europe," by Tirana Hassan, Amnesty International, January 18, 2016. Reprinted by permission.

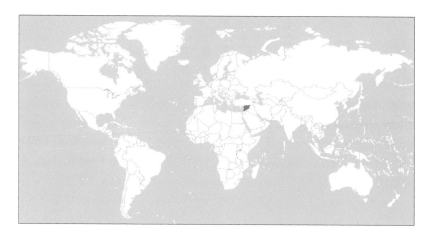

The organization interviewed 40 refugee women and girls in northern Europe last month who traveled from Turkey to Greece and then across the Balkans. All the women described feeling threatened and unsafe during the journey. Many reported that in almost all of the countries they passed through they experienced physical abuse and financial exploitation, being groped or pressured to have sex by smugglers, security staff or other refugees.

"After living through the horrors of the war in Iraq and Syria these women have risked everything to find safety for themselves and their children. But from the moment they begin this journey they are again exposed to violence and exploitation, with little support or protection," said Tirana Hassan, Amnesty International's Crisis Response director.

Women and girls traveling alone and those accompanied only by their children felt particularly under threat in transit areas and camps in Hungary, Croatia and Greece, where they were forced to sleep alongside hundreds of refugee men. In some instances women left the designated areas to sleep in the open on the beach because they felt safer there.

Women also reported having to use the same bathroom and shower facilities as men. One woman told Amnesty International that in a reception centre in Germany some refugee men would watch women as they went to the bathroom. Some women took extreme measures such as not eating or drinking to avoid having to go to the toilet where they felt unsafe.

"If this humanitarian crisis was unfolding anywhere else in the world we would expect immediate practical steps to be taken to protect groups most at risk of abuse, such as women traveling alone and female-headed families. At a minimum, this would include setting up single sex, well-lit toilet facilities and separate safe sleeping areas. These women and their children have fled some of the world's most dangerous areas and it is shameful that they are still at risk on European soil," said Tirana Hassan.

"While governments and those who provide services to refugees have started to put measures in place to help refugees, they must up their game. More steps need to be taken to ensure that refugee women, especially those most at risk, are identified and special processes and services are put in place to ensure that their basic rights, safety and security are protected."

Amnesty International researchers spoke to seven pregnant women who described a lack of food and basic healthcare as well as being crushed at border and transit points during the journey.

One Syrian woman was pregnant and breastfeeding her young daughter when she made the journey with her husband, said she was too scared to sleep in camps in Greece knowing she was surrounded by men. She also described how she went for several days without eating.

A dozen of the women interviewed said that they had been touched, stroked or leered at in European transit camps. One 22-year-old Iraqi woman told Amnesty International that when she was in Germany a uniformed security guard offered to give her some clothes in exchange for "spending time alone" with him.

"Nobody should have to take these dangerous routes in the first place. The best way to avoid abuses and exploitation by smugglers is for European governments to allow safe and legal routes from the outset. For those who have no other choice, it is completely unacceptable that their passage across Europe exposes them to further humiliation, uncertainty and insecurity," said Tirana Hassan.

Additional Testimonies

Sexual exploitation by smugglers

Smugglers target women who are traveling alone knowing they are more vulnerable. When they lacked the financial resources to pay for their journey smugglers would often try to coerce them into having sex.

At least three women said that smugglers and those working with the smugglers' network harassed them or others, and offered them a discounted trip or a shorter wait to get on the boat across the Mediterranean, in exchange for sex.

Hala, a 23-year-old woman from Aleppo told Amnesty International:

> "At the hotel in Turkey, one of the men working with the smuggler, a Syrian man, said if I sleep with him, I will not pay or pay less. Of course I said no, it was disgusting. The same happened in Jordan to all of us.
>
> My friend who came with me from Syria ran out of money in Turkey, so the smuggler's assistant offered her to have sex with him [in exchange for a place on a boat]; she of course said no, and couldn't leave Turkey, so she's staying there."

Nahla, a 20-year old from Syria told Amnesty International:

> "The smuggler was harassing me. He tried to touch me a couple of times. Only when my male cousin was around he did not come close. I was very afraid, especially that we hear stories along the way of women who can't afford the smugglers who would be given the option to sleep with the smugglers for a discount."

Harassment and living in constant fear

All of the women told Amnesty International that they were constantly scared during the journey across Europe. Women traveling alone were not only targeted by smugglers but felt physically threatened when forced to sleep in facilities with hundreds of single men. Several women also reported being beaten or verbally abused by security officers in Greece, Hungary and Slovenia.

Reem, a 20-year-old from Syria who was traveling with her 15-year-old cousin:

> "I never got the chance to sleep in settlements. I was too scared that anyone would touch me. The tents were all mixed and I witnessed violence... I felt safer in movements, especially on the bus, the only place I could shut my eyes and sleep. In the camps we are so prone to being touched, and women can't really complain and they don't want to cause issues to disrupt their trip."

Violence by police and conditions in the transit camps

Women and girls reported filthy conditions in a number of transit camps, where food was limited and pregnant women in particular found little or no support. Women also reported that toilet facilities were often squalid and women felt unsafe as some sanitary facilities were not segregated by sex. For example, in at least two instances women were watched by men at the facility when they accessed the bathrooms. Some women also experienced direct violence from other refugees, as well as by police, particularly when tensions rose in cramped conditions and security forces intervened.

Rania, a 19-year-old pregnant woman from Syria, told Amnesty International about her experience in Hungary:

> "The police then moved us to another place, which was even worse. It was full of cages and there wasn't any air coming in. We were locked up. We stayed there for two days. We received two meals a day. The toilets were worse than in the other camps, I feel like they mean to keep the toilets like that to make us suffer.
>
> On our second day there, the police hit a Syrian woman from Aleppo because she begged the police to let her go... Her sister tried to defend her, she spoke English, was told that if she doesn't shut up they will hit her like her sister. A similar

situation happened to an Iranian woman the next day because she asked for extra food for her kids."

Maryam, a 16-year-old from Syria:

(In Greece) "People started screaming and shouting, so the police attacked us and was hitting everyone with sticks. They hit me on my arm with a stick. They even hit younger kids. They hit everyone even on the head. I got dizzy and I fell, people were stepping on me. I was crying and was separated from my mother. They called my name and I was with my mother. I showed them my arm and a police officer saw my arm and laughed, I asked for a doctor, they asked me and my mother to leave."

Living in a War Zone May Be Better Than Refugee Life

Bethan Staton

In the following viewpoint, Bethan Staton notes that thousands of Syrian refugees are returning to their home country. This is despite the fact that many of them expect to face death in war-torn Syria. Staton claims this trend shows the difficulty of refugee life, particularly in Jordan. Syrian refugees there cannot legally work and they live in extreme poverty. Some now view the danger of Syria as preferable to the poverty of Jordan. Bethan Staton is a journalist based in the Middle East.

As you read, consider the following questions:

1. How many Syrian refugees were registered in Jordan at the time of this article?
2. What percentage of Syrian refugees in Jordan were considering leaving Jordan?
3. How much money do Syrian refugees in Jordan receive to buy food for a month?

Z AATARI, Jordan — It was four years ago, when war broke out in Homs, that Khaled al-Nibeeti and his family fled their home for the first time.

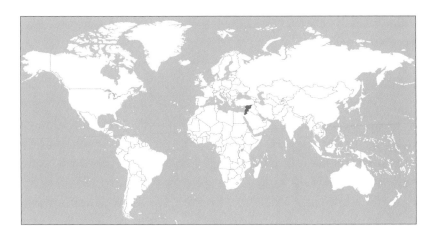

They traveled to Palmyra, then to the desert nearby. When airstrikes there made them too afraid to light their tent at night they left Syria altogether, spending their last money on checkpoint taxes and a rented car to reach Jordan.

In Jordan, they moved from Zaatari refugee camp to the overcrowded city of Mafraq, eventually finding safety in Zaatari village, six miles from the Syrian border. They stayed there for a year and a half.

This week, they'll travel again. But at a time when hundreds of thousands of refugees are making their way to Europe, this family is doing the unthinkable: returning to the war-ravaged country they once fled.

"I'd prefer to die in Syria," Khaled al-Nibeeti told GlobalPost, rocking his 1-year-old son Mohammed to a fitful sleep. The baby has been ill for seven days, but the family can't afford to pay for transport to see a doctor or get medicine. "It's better for me to die in Syria than live here, when life in Jordan is so hard."

Al-Nibeeti is one of thousands of Syrian refugees returning to their home country — a decision that increasing numbers have been driven to in recent months. This week he'll sell his belongings, speak with the UNHCR at Zaatari camp, and take his family to board the bus to the border. It's a journey with no return ticket and an uncertain end: Khaled knows his brother, who lives near

Palmyra, will help him out, but he has no idea what dangers might prevent him from reaching his destination safely, if at all.

"We're not thinking about the future," he said. "We're thinking just about how we live day to day. Here, there is no future."

According to the United Nations, more than 100 Syrians have been leaving Jordan for Syria every day in recent months. They're fleeing poverty, frustration and hopelessness: the sharp end of a humanitarian crisis that has dragged on for more than four years. With some 630,000 Syrian refugees currently registered in Jordan, the resources to provide them with food, shelter and support have been thinly stretched for too long. Now, aid cuts mean the most vulnerable are struggling to survive.

"Before, there was always something. People would come with a food box, a bit of help," al-Nibeeti said. "Now there's nothing. We go to the supermarket and we just buy everything on credit. There's nothing new."

The gravity of the crisis facing al-Nibeeti and others like him is perhaps best illustrated by the World Food Program's rapidly shrinking allowance for refugees. In the past, Syrians received 24 Jordanian dinars (about $34) per person, per month to buy food. By September, that had been cut completely for 229,000 people, and reduced to just 10 dinars for the most vulnerable.

The aid is the only source of sustenance for many refugees. Although it's been reinstated this month, al-Nibeeti says he only receives enough assistance to feed his family for about ten days.

For the vast majority of Syrians who, like al-Nibeeti, live outside the camps, the situation is most serious. The cost of living is high in Jordan: Many struggle to make rent, and it's now commonplace for families to take children out of school so they can work. An estimated 86 percent of urban Syrian refugees are living below the Jordanian poverty line.

"What people don't always understand is that the World Food Program cuts coincided with cuts in other organizations — smaller NGOS that have been helping the refugees out with rent and so on," Shada Moghraby, a spokesperson for the WFP, said. "Needless to say, with the impact of the cuts we've seen families resorting to emergency coping mechanisms. We've seen early childhood marriage, begging."

Among refugees poverty has led to despair; constantly changing news about the help they can access, delivered by text message, is leading many to feel angry with the UN. In the clean, sparsely furnished tent where al-Nibeeti lives with his wife and five children, he and his neighbors debate rumors that food aid for Syrians will be cut altogether.

"If the food allowance stops for good, you won't find any refugees in Jordan," Khaled Faris argues. For him, returning to Syria still means death, and going back to a war zone is unthinkable. But he, too, is looking for a way out of Jordan, preferably to Europe.

An hour's drive from Zaatari, Um Faisal is making the same decision. Her home in Amman is almost empty now: Three suitcases surrounded by scattered belongings sit waiting for the trip she and her two sons will make to Istanbul at the beginning of November. After that, she says, she's not sure what she will do.

"The life here is so difficult. We look poverty in the face. There's so many problems. We don't have any work, no support. We can't produce anything. We don't have anything here," she says. "We are like the living dead."

After landing in Turkey, Um Faisal has no idea what she will do aside from connecting with other family members. "You tell me, what should we do? We'll take anything." The vague plan is to head for Reyhanli, close to the Syrian border. It would be better to stay in the desert, she says, than come back to Jordan.

Poverty is only part of the problem. Both Um Faisal and al-Nibeeti only stayed in Zaatari, Jordan's largest camp, for a few hours — they say being trapped in the overcrowded tent city, where crime is reportedly rife, was unbearable. But in Jordan's towns and cities, they're unable to work legally and see no opportunity to improve their circumstances.

Once he's left for Syria al-Nibeeti won't be able to return to Jordan, but he remains single-mindedly committed to the dangerous journey. "I'm out of my mind. I'm up awake all night until the morning, all the time I'm thinking of what I can do for my family, how I'll live. There's nothing I can do."

Last month, UN reports indicated that the flow of refugees back to Syria stabilized — a development related partly to the heightened civilian risk brought by Russian air strikes in Syria. Whether the trend will continue as conditions worsen into the winter, however, remains to be seen. In a survey of 500 refugees released by the UN in September, 49 percent said they were considering leaving Jordan. The majority of those wanted to leave because they had no means to survive, and 13 percent said they'd go because they saw no future in the host country.

"There's nothing here. There's no help with the food. There's no help with the family. There's no work. The baby's been sick for seven days, and he can't get the food he needs," al-Nibeeti's wife Fatat explained. She's frightened to travel back to Syria, but with her husband so committed to the move she sees few options.

"There's no future in Syria, in Syria there is only death," she said. "But it's better to die in Syria than to live here in the dirt."

Periodical and Internet Sources Bibliography

The following articles have been selected to supplement the diverse views presented in this chapter.

Jess Bidgood, "Ailing Vermont Town Pins Hopes on Mideast Refugees," The New York Times, January 2, 2017. https://www.nytimes.com/2017/01/02/us/syria-iraq-refugees-vermont-rutland-plan.html

Louiza Chekhar, "No place for children," British Red Cross, 2016. https://www.redcross.org.uk/~/media/BritishRedCross/Documents/What%20we%20do/Refugee%20support/No%20place%20for%20children.pdf

Russell Goldman, "Trump's Immigration Ban Blocks Children Most in Need of Aid," The New York Times, January 31, 2017. https://www.nytimes.com/2017/01/31/world/middleeast/trump-immigration-ban-children.html

Stephanie Nebehay, "Natural disasters forced 20 million from their homes in 2014: report," Reuters, July 20, 2015. http://www.reuters.com/article/us-climatechange-migrants-idUSKCN0PU1M120150720

Ahmed Rashid, "Viewpoint: Why Afghan refugees are facing a humanitarian catastrophe," October 12, 2016. http://www.bbc.com/news/world-asia-37607785

Amanda Sakuma, What's in a name? Migrant vs. refugee vs. illegal immigrant," MSNBC, May 19, 2016. http://www.msnbc.com/msnbc/whats-name-migrant-vs-refugee-vs-illegal-immigrant

Alastair Sloan, "Britain rejecting child refugees is no surprise," Al Jazeera, February 4, 2017. Http://www.aljazeera.com/indepth/opinion/2017/02/britain-rejecting-child-refugees-surprise-170214081706478.html

"Ten countries host half of world's refugees: report," Al Jazeera News And News Agencies, 2016. http://www.aljazeera.com/news/2016/10/ten-countries-host-world-refugees-report-161004042014076.html

UNCHR, "Frequently asked questions on climate change and disaster displacement," United Nations High Commissioner for Refugees, November 6, 2016.

http://www.unhcr.org/en-us/news/latest/2016/11/581f52dc4/ frequently-asked-questions-climate-change-disaster- displacement.html

World Atlas, Which Country Produces The Most Refugees?" World Atlas, 2016. http://www.worldatlas.com/articles/the-origins-of-the-world-s-refugees.html

World Humanitarian Summit secretariat, "Restoring Humanity: Synthesis of the Consultation Process for the World Humanitarian Summit," United Nations, 2015. https://www.worldhumanitariansummit.org/key-documents#major-reports-linking

CHAPTER 2

Whose Responsibility Are Migrants and Refugees?

Refugee Crisis Causes Strife and Disagreement in Europe

Andreas Liljeheden

In the following viewpoint, Andreas Liljeheden claims that the European Union is divided on how to handle the refugee crisis. Sources criticize individual countries and the EU as a whole for the response to refugees. Some solutions have been offered, but critics suggest they do not go far enough. The article paints a picture of an inadequate European response to the refugee situation. Andreas Liljeheden is a journalist based in Belgium.

As you read, consider the following questions:

1. Which country in particular has been called out as not living up to EU ideals in accepting refugees?
2. How much money is supposed to be given by the EU and member states to help the UN handle Syrian refugees?
3. How did better funding for border control help save lives?

The refugee crisis has increased tensions in the EU as member states have blamed each other for not doing enough to handle the massive flow of refugee arrivals. European solidarity and values have been questioned. But even if the EU is struggling to deal with the crisis, Europe has done little compared to poorer countries close to Syria. And civil society groups still accuse the EU of blocking borders rather than helping people in need.

"Refugee Crisis Divides EU Countries," by Andreas Liljeheden, Euranet Plus, September 24, 2015. Reprinted by permission. Andreas Liljeheden ©Euranet Plus (Brussels).

This year, Europe has seen a massive flow of refugees reaching European shores fleeing war, persecution and poverty. Thousands have died on the way. It is described as the worst humanitarian crises in Europe since World War II.

EU countries haven't been able to cope with the situation. The European asylum system has proven to be flawed, member states have pointed fingers, closed borders and pushed refugees to their neighbours rather than working together towards a common solution.

At an extraordinary summit on migration in Brussels on September 23, the EU heads of state or government tried to display a united façade. But in the press room the word spread that German Chancellor Angela Merkel had given the Hungarian Prime Minister Viktor Orbán a good talking-to during the evening for trying to protect the country's border with a barbed wire fence and military force.

French President François Hollande went further, questioning Hungary's place in the EU.

"Europe is built on values and principles. Those who don't share these values, those who don't want to respect these principles, should ask themselves about their place in the European Union," said Hollande during the summit in Brussels.

The day before, Hungary had been overruled by a majority of EU member states on relocation of refugees.

When the justice and home affairs ministers voted on the relocation of 120,000 refugees, Hungary, Romania, Slovakia and the Czech Republic voted against while Finland abstained. The annexes of the meeting conclusions contained numbers of refugees that member states had to accept. The 120,000 comes on top of the previously agreed relocation of 40,000. In total, the relocation mechanism amounts to 160,000.

Thus, the countries who voted against will in practice be forced to accept refugees. And this also means that people fleeing war will have to seek asylum in countries where they are not welcome.

The Slovakian Prime Minister Robert Fico simply refused to accept the decision. Shortly after the vote he said that mandatory quotas would not be implemented in his country as long as he was prime minister and he also threatened to challenge the decision in court.

The political family of Fico, the European Socialists and Democrats, is now considering to suspend him from the group, saying he has "embarrassed the whole progressive family."

The harsh comments show how divided EU member states are in how to solve the refugee crisis. One who has called for more solidarity is António Guterres, UN High Commissioner for Refugees and former prime minister of Portugal.

In a debate in the European Parliament he specifically mentioned Hungary, whose minister not only voted against the relocation, but also declined the EU offer to have 54,000 refugees relocated from its territory.

Guterres pointed at Hungary in 1956 when hundreds of thousands of Hungarians fled dictatorship to neighbouring countries like Austria. At that time, 140,000 were relocated to other countries in Europe and elsewhere.

"And relocation into other European countries took less than three months. At that time, European integration was starting, there was no European Union, but at least that part of the union that could be united was united to protect the Hungarian victims of oppression and dictatorship," Guterres said.

"Now unfortunately today we have a European Union but Europe is no longer united. Europe is divided," he concluded.

Poor countries take more responsibility

Eugenio Ambrosi, regional director for the EU at the International Organization for Migration (IOM), thinks the vote in the council, where some member states were forced to participate in the relocation scheme, sends a negative signal to countries outside Europe. The EU demonstrates that it is not ready to unite on sharing global responsibility while asking others for help.

"The EU is asking the cooperation of other regions of the world to manage this flow. And therefore the fact that they are unable to cooperate among themselves effectively makes the case of asking for cooperation from other regions far more weaker than it would be," Ambrosi said in an interview with Euranet Plus.

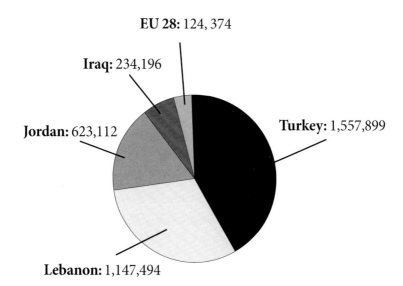

Syrian Refugees 2014

EU 28: 124, 374

Iraq: 234,196

Jordan: 623,112

Turkey: 1,557,899

Lebanon: 1,147,494

Many of the refugees that are coming to Europe are Syrians fleeing the war that started in 2011 following the Arab spring protests. Since then more than four million people have left the country. As the graph below shows, most of them have not come to Europe, but to neighbouring countries.

The numbers are annual figures from 2014, but the overall picture hasn't changed. Europe has taken on a very small portion of the total number of fleeing Syrians.

EU Commission President Jean-Claude Juncker argued in his annual state of the union speech on September 9 that the number of refugees arriving in Europe corresponds to only 0.11 percent of the total population, a very small number compared to the Syrian neighbours such as Lebanon.

"Refugees [in Lebanon] represent 25 percent of the population in a country which has only one fifth of the wealth we do enjoy in the European Union. Who are we that we are never making this kind of comparisons. Who are we?" asked Juncker, whose statement was applauded in the EU Parliament.

More money for Syria

In the summit on September 23, EU leaders agreed to support Syria and its neighbouring countries. At least one billion euros is to be given from member states and the EU budget in support for the work of the UN in the region.

This goes hand in hand with the support from the Commission, which has launched a regional fund for Syria, as well as a trust fund for Africa to tackle the root causes of migration. The Commission has put aside 1.8 billion euros from the EU budget for this purpose.

On September 15 the EU Commissioner for Foreign Affairs, Federica Mogherini, impatiently urged member states to also chip in to the Africa trust fund.

"I am waiting for member states to give consistent, significant contributions to this trust fund. Not in one year. Tomorrow. The day after tomorrow. For the moment that's it, 1.8 billion euros on the European Union budget. We sent a letter last week to all member states, to all ministers, inviting them to contribute. I expect contributions to come in the next hours, not months, hours," Mogherini said.

More than a week later, only two member states, France and Spain, have confirmed their participation in writing, one EU source told Euranet Plus, adding that other member states had "indicated interest to participate."

"But we don't expect their financial contributions to be made public before the Valletta Summit in November," the source said.

The formal decision on the fund will be taken at the EU-Africa summit in Malta on November 11 and 12.

One million refugees to arrive in Europe

Civil society groups have continuously questioned the European response to the refugee crisis. Neither the measures taken nor the proposed actions, which include a permanent relocation scheme, a list of safe countries of origin, improved asylum procedures and better border surveillance, are enough, they argue.

The agreed emergency scheme, where 160,000 refugees are to be relocated from Italy, Greece and possibly other member states during the coming years, is small given the high numbers of current and expected arrivals.

In Greece alone over 360,000 refugees have arrived since the beginning of the year, according to the IOM. 491,005 have crossed the sea towards Greece and Italy combined. The OECD is expecting that this number will reach one million by the end of the 2014. The relocation for this year and the next is expected to be 106,000 – roughly ten percent of the expected arrivals for 2015.

The dire situation in countries like Greece and Italy, where refugees arrive by thousand per day, could be relieved by a permanent relocation mechanism that the Commission is pushing for. But given the difficulty among member states to agree on a temporary relocation of 160,000, a permanent scheme seems distant.

John Dalhuisen, Amnesty International's Director of Europe, said in a press statement that "the relocation figures won't significantly relieve the pressure on frontline states. Without much more concrete and immediate assistance to these countries, the chaotic tragic scenes we have witnessed in recent weeks, will only continue and likely worsen."

As many other NGOs, Amnesty International is also questioning the overall EU policy to handle the refugee crisis. They say that the agreed and proposed measures focus too much on simply keeping migrants and refugees away rather than helping people in need. The cost of this European policy, they argue, is not measured in euros, but human lives.

Médecins Sans Frontières claim that the refugee crisis in Europe is a tragedy directly linked to the policies pursued by the EU.

After the Italian led search and rescue operation Mare Nostrum ended in the fall of 2014, the number of lives lost in the Mediterranean sky rocketed.

In April this year, more than 1,200 people died trying to make it to European shores. The EU then decided to increase the resources for the union's own border control agency, Frontex. Since then, 122,000 people have been saved in the Mediterranean, according to the Commission. Though the numbers have not been confirmed by Frontex, they show the clear link between Mediterranean rescue operations and decreased deaths.

The Commission has now pledged more money from member states in order to increase the border surveillance and control. The EU Migration Commissioner, Dimitris Avramopoulos, will put forward a proposal before the end of the year that is supposed to transform Frontex into a proper coast guard. The proposal is said to include a 54 percent budget increase for the agency in 2016. Also member states have expressed their willingness to provide personnel and equipment.

But civil society groups are not satisfied. Instead they call on the EU to provide safe and legal routes for refugees into Europe, for instance by giving humanitarian visas in third countries outside the

EU. That way people seeking asylum wouldn't have to risk their lives being shipped over to Europe by smugglers on unseaworthy boats.

At the IOM, Ambrosi agrees that better border management is needed. But he stresses that it has to go hand in hand with other measures such as better reception of asylum seekers and resettlement from countries neighbouring Syria.

To simply close the border, for instance by building barbed wire fences as in Hungary, will not work, he argues.

"Simply trying to seal the border doesn't work. The mass of people is too big, the drivers that make these people move are too strong. They are not going to stop in front of a fence. It will just make things more dangerous."

Christians Should Support Opening Borders to More Refugees

David Hollenbach

In the following viewpoint, David Hollenbach addresses the refugee crisis from an ethical standpoint. He suggests that Christians have special duties toward suffering people, including refugees. He notes that some philosophers believe borders should be eliminated but does not himself make that claim. Hollenbach believes that people may have additional responsibilities to family members and fellow citizens, but that this does not eliminate their responsibility to strangers from other countries. He states that rich countries, in particular, should accept more refugees. David Hollenbach is a Jesuit priest, university professor, and human rights advocate.

As you read, consider the following questions:

1. Has the number of international migrants been increasing or decreasing?
2. How many migrants were displaced by war or other violent conflict in 2015?
3. What percentage of refugees are hosted by developing countries?

Migration has been occurring throughout human history, since early humans left eastern Africa for Arabia and the rest of the world about 60,000 years ago. People have always been seeking to improve their lives or to escape war, oppression, famine and other threats to their well-being by moving. In recent decades, however, migration has been dramatically increasing. In 2013, the number of international migrants worldwide reached 232 million, up from 154 million in 1990 and from 76 million in 1960.

Many modern migrants are fleeing war and conflict in places like Syria, Iraq, South Sudan, Central African Republic and elsewhere. In 2015 the U.N. High Commissioner for Refugees reported that the number of people displaced by war, intrastate strife and human rights violations had reached 59.5 million in 2014, 8.3 million more than a year earlier. This was the highest number of displaced persons ever recorded. The number of deaths from conflict and disasters also remains distressingly high. In the eastern part of the Democratic Republic of Congo alone, from 2005 to 2015 over five million persons died due to conflict, chiefly from disease and malnutrition brought about by the fighting. Sadly the protection of people from severe threats to their humanity remains a distant goal.

Well-Founded Fears

A refugee is a specific kind of migrant. The 1951 United Nations' Refugee Convention defines a refugee as a person who, "owing to well-founded fear of being persecuted for reasons of race, religion, nationality, membership of a particular social group or political opinion, is outside the country of his nationality." Refugees have little or no choice about their movement. Because of the persecution they face, their most basic human rights are on the line. The phrase "forced migrants" has recently been coined to take into account the fact that religious, ethnic or social persecution is not the only coercive pressure that drives people from their homes. They can be forced from home yet still remain in their own country as "internally displaced persons." And people escaping extreme poverty may have a moral claim for admission to another country as urgent as a refugee's claim for asylum.

What can we say about our responsibilities in the face of this suffering? As the number of refugees seeking asylum from grave threats has risen, secular political philosophers, like Joseph Carens of the University of Toronto, and refugee scholars, like Philip Marfleet of the University of East London in the United Kingdom, have argued that the time has come to consider making borders fully open to migration and to granting asylum to all people who are fleeing from persecution, conflict or disaster. In a similar spirit, several years ago Martha Nussbaum, a University of Chicago philosopher, argued that the cosmopolitan community of all human beings has primacy over narrower communities defined in terms of nationality, ethnicity or religion. Indeed she called nationality a "morally irrelevant" characteristic of personhood.

This support for open borders can be given Christian religious backing. Christopher Hale, executive director of Catholics in Alliance for the Common Good and a Catholic cultural commentator for *Time* magazine, affirms that "in Jesus Christ, there are no borders." This stance has biblical roots. In the Gospel of Matthew, for example, just after Jesus' birth he was driven from home with Mary and Joseph by King Herod's effort to destroy him as a threat to his regime. Anachronistically, we could say that since Jesus was fleeing persecution across a border, he met the contemporary international convention's definition of a refugee. Also in Matthew's Gospel, Jesus teaches that on the Day of Judgment one's salvation or damnation will be determined by whether one has welcomed the hungry, the thirsty and, most relevant here, the stranger (Mt 25:40). Thus Christians should recognize their special duties to suffering people who are not members of their own communities, including migrants and refugees.

Jesus' inclusive teachings echo affirmations from the Book of Genesis that all people have been created in the image of God and are thus brothers and sisters in a single human family, no matter what their nationality or ethnicity. Every person is created with a worth that reaches across national borders. The universality of human dignity led Pope John XXIII to insist that "the fact that one is a citizen of a particular state does not detract in any way from his membership in the human family as a whole, nor from his citizenship in the world community."

The question, of course, is whether this philosophical and Christian universalism means that state borders have no moral relevance. In fact, the issue is more complex. An appreciation of the common humanity of all people must not only support the unity of the human family but must also respect the differences among peoples, cultures and nations. An exclusive stress on what we have in common will have difficulty explaining why being forced from home, either as a refugee or within one's own country, has such negative moral significance.

We need, therefore, a more differentiated approach to how responsibilities reach across borders than the stress on the unity of the human family, taken alone, can provide. In her recent writings Professor Nussbaum now draws on Grotius and Kant to argue that people exercise their freedom and express their dignity when they join together to shape the institutions of their own nation state. Protecting the independence of accountable states is thus a way of protecting human dignity.

Weighing Obligations

In a similar way, though Christianity requires universal respect for all persons, it also requires respect for their distinctive identities. St. Augustine and St. Thomas Aquinas both affirm a Christian duty to love all humans as our neighbors. At the same time, they recognize that there is an order of priorities among our loves (an ordo amoris). Those with whom we have special relationships, like our family or our fellow citizens, deserve distinctive forms of treatment as an expression of our love for them. Christian love therefore requires both universal respect for all and distinctive concern for those with whom we have special relationships. Christian ethics affirms that one has special duties to one's co-

World Humanitarian Summit

The world's first-ever World Humanitarian Summit took place May 23–24, 2016 in Istanbul. … The Agenda for Humanity outlines the five core responsibilities that the summit centered on:

1. "Global leadership to prevent and end conflict." The first core responsibility proposes responding quickly to crises and investing in risk analysis, political unity, and peace building to prevent conflicts from occurring. Manmade conflict accounts for 80 percent of humanitarian aid that is sent, according to the WHS Executive Summary Report. Investing in conflict prevention would save billions of dollars and lives.

2. "Uphold the norms that safeguard humanity." The second core responsibility addresses the need to recommit to rules of war and speak out against violations. When bombs or explosives are used in populated areas, 90 percent of people that are killed or injured are civilians, according to the WHS Executive Summary Report. This responsibility presents the launch of a global campaign to stop violations of the human rights law, while investing in ways to increase adherence and accountability.

3. "Leave no one behind." The third core responsibility is dedicated to reaching everyone affected by crises, risk and vulnerability. According to the WHS Report, 60 million people are forcibly displaced, and there is a severe lack of funding in humanitarian aid. This responsibility commits to empowering marginalized groups, addressing displacement and supporting migrants.

4. "Changing people's lives – from delivering aid to ending need." The fourth core responsibility is centered on shifting the priority from delivering aid to ending the need for aid. Reinforcing the idea that support should be drawn from within, this commitment advises employing local solutions and empowering local systems that already work instead of replacing them with international aid.

5. "Invest in humanity." The fifth core responsibility commits to political, institutional and financial investments in stability and local systems. It proposes to decrease the funding gap and improve the efficiency of aid. The World Humanitarian Summit comes at a critical time in history – a time when the U.N. estimates that the number of people displaced has not been as high since World War II.

"World Humanitarian Summit Commits to Shared Responsibility," by Erica Rawles, July 29, 2016.

citizens, just as one does to one's siblings and friends. At the same time, Christian ethics forbids actions and policies that in effect treat those of other countries who are in grave need as nonpersons.

The mass movement of people in our world today calls us to reflect carefully on the relative weights of the obligations and rights that arise from our common humanity and from our distinctive identities. Let me suggest several priorities among these duties and rights. We should begin by reaffirming the United Nations' 1951 Refugee Convention's affirmation that refugees fleeing persecution should have a high-priority claim to be granted asylum in another country.

Refugees are people who have virtually no alternative except flight from home. In almost all cases their choice is either migration or loss of basic human rights, in many cases even the right to life. Thus in all cases where a country has the resources to admit refugees without severely jeopardizing the life and well-being of its own citizens, it ought to do so, granting asylum to the refugees at its borders.

In addition, we should insist with the Refugee Convention that refugees have a right not to be subject to forcible return (refoulement) to regions where they face serious threats to their lives and freedoms. The priority of non-refoulement of refugees is grounded both in Christian respect for the dignity of every person and in the wisdom formed by political experience.

It is clear that wealthy countries like those of Europe and North America have the resources needed to grant asylum to refugees from countries like Syria and South Sudan today. Chancellor Angela Merkel took the right path when she decided to relax Germany's borders to all those fleeing the chaos of Syria.

When Prime Minister David Cameron of the United Kingdom announced that his country would grant asylum to 20,000 people over the next five years, however, he was appropriately reminded that Lebanon had admitted that many Syrians over the previous two weekends. Indeed, developing countries today host 86 percent of the world's refugees, the highest percentage in more than two decades, and the very poorest countries among them are providing asylum to 25 percent of the global total. Thus the rich nations of the North have a duty to admit a considerably larger number of asylum seekers than they do now and an even greater duty to assist these less-developed countries that are already hosting most of the world's refugees. Sadly, the funds being provided for this burden-sharing by the North fall far short of what is needed.

For Rich Countries, Special Responsibilities

It is also clear that in wealthy nations like those of the United States, Europe and Australia, much of the negative attitude toward migrants and refugees is grounded in a mixture of racially driven xenophobia and a mistaken fear that refugees may be terrorists. Dislike of the needy stranger, especially when motivated by racial or religious stereotypes, is clearly contrary to core principles of Christianity and to the secular norms of a human rights ethic as well. The asylum needed by refugees should be a top priority as we determine how to combine loyalty to our own community and to those from other societies. Balancing these loyalties requires that we work to overcome exclusionary, xenophobic attitudes.

A further priority arises from the special duty a rich country that has contributed to the economic deprivation of a poor country can have toward migrants from that country, especially if they are fleeing the dangers of war. For example, European powers that benefited from colonizing regions of Africa or Asia without contributing to their development have significant duties to be open to refugees and other migrants from these regions. Thus France and the United Kingdom have duties to migrants from their former colonies that they probably do not have to migrants in general. Economic benefit through forms of exploitation other than formal colonization can create similar duties. For example, the political and economic history of the United States in nations like Guatemala and Haiti creates special duties to admit people from those countries, especially refugees fleeing political persecution.

A country with a history of military involvement in the life of another country may also have special obligations. The United States recognized its special duty to receive refugees from Vietnam following the end of the Vietnam War in 1975. And though U.S. military engagement in Iraq was not the sole cause of the displacement of many Iraqis, the U.S. intervention was the occasion of the huge forced migration of Iraqis that followed.

As the Harvard political scientist Stephen Walt commented in the aftermath of the terror attacks in Paris on Nov. 13, if the United States and its allies had not invaded Iraq in 2003, there would almost certainly be no Islamic State today. Thus the United States and its allies in Iraq have especially strong duties to admit refugees seeking asylum from Iraq and Syria, as well as others fleeing the economic deprivation caused by war in the region. They also have serious responsibilities to help rebuild the political and economic life whose destruction has been the source of the huge movement of Iraqi and Syrian people.

There are no doubt additional grounds for a country to grant priority to the admission of migrants from a particular background when not all can be received. These suggestions indicate the direction we should be moving today. Indeed, the most fundamental criterion for determining our priorities should be our duty to support the basic human dignity of those whose lives and basic human rights are severely threatened. As Pope Francis has repeatedly stressed, duties to refugees are duties to our brothers and sisters in the human family and, we Christians believe, duties to Christ. We are urgently challenged to live up to these duties.

The US Must Help Fix the Crisis It Caused

Marjorie Cohn

In the following viewpoint, Marjorie Cohn claims that the United States played a role in creating refugees from the Middle East. Therefore, the author believes that the US has a moral obligation to take in more Syrian refugees. She claims that rich countries should be doing more to help refugees, both in terms of accepting more immigrants and in providing more money. Marjorie Cohn is a lawyer and former law professor who lectures on international human rights and US foreign-policy.

As you read, consider the following questions:

1. How many refugees were said to be created by the US invasion of Iraq?
2. How is the definition of refugee changing?
3. What solution does the author suggest to end the conflict in Syria?

"The US Has a Duty to the Syrian Refugees," by Marjorie Cohn, Truthdig, LLC, September 22, 2015. Reprinted by permission.

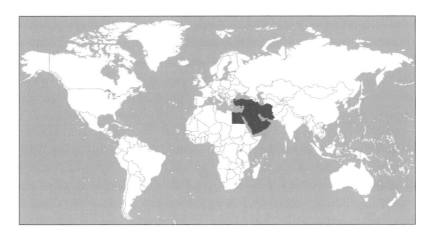

M any of us are familiar with the Emma Lazarus poem on a plaque at the base of the Statue of Liberty:

> "Give me your tired, your poor,
> Your huddled masses yearning to breathe free,
> The wretched refuse of your teeming shore.
> Send these, the homeless, tempest-tost to me,
> I lift my lamp beside the golden door!"

These words, written in the late 19th century, depicted the United States as a refuge for people who had crossed the Atlantic seeking a new home and a better life than they experienced in the places they left behind. The current massive humanitarian crisis in the Middle East, which has created a flood of refugees exiting Syria, obliges our country to live up to the welcome promised in that poem.

With George W. Bush's invasion and occupation of Iraq, which led to the birth of Islamic State, the U.S. government played a significant role in destabilizing the Middle East. The United States and its allies—including Saudi Arabia and Turkey—have trained, financed and supplied weapons to forces fighting the government of Bashar al-Assad in Syria. This has exacerbated the refugee crisis we are now witnessing.

History professor and author Juan Cole wrote that the U.S. invasion of Iraq created 4 million refugees, about one-sixth of

Iraq's population. But "the U.S. took in only a few thousand Iraqi refugees after causing all that trouble," he noted. The United States must do better with the Syrian refugees.

Former Secretary of State Colin Powell, speaking about the U.S. invasion of Iraq, famously said, "If you break it, you own it."

Yet President Barack Obama pledged to lift the U.S. lamp to only 10,000 of the 4 million refugees fleeing Syria. After fielding criticism of the United States for taking so few, Secretary of State John Kerry announced that the U.S. would accept 185,000 refugees over the next two years. But this figure reflects the total number from many countries; there is no indication the administration will accept more than 10,000 from Syria.

The United States has a moral obligation, and perhaps a legal one, to accept many of the Syrian refugees. Evolving international norms suggest that all the countries of the world have a duty to provide refuge to those who have fled their homeland to escape persecution or war. Because the United States has 28 percent of the world's wealth, we should take at least 28 percent of the refugees, according to Phyllis Bennis of the Institute for Policy Studies. That would amount to about 350,000 people. And she says the United States should immediately pay 28 percent of the United Nations' refugee relief request, about $5.5 billion, to support nearly 6 million refugees from Syria and nearby countries through the end of 2015.

The 1951 Refugee Convention and its 1967 Protocol define a refugee as someone outside his or her country who has a well-founded fear of persecution on account of race, religion, nationality, membership in a particular social group or political opinion. Due to the fear of persecution, he or she is unable or unwilling to remain in his or her country of origin.

Although many Syrian refugees may meet this definition, many others don't because they fled to escape the violence of the armed conflict ravaging their country, not necessarily to avoid persecution.

Some scholars, however, think a much broader definition of "refugee" is evolving under conventional and customary international law. For example, William Thomas Worster wrote in the Berkeley Journal of International Law that a refugee could be a person who has a well-founded fear of "a threat to life, security or liberty due to events seriously disturbing public order" throughout his or her country—and because of that fear is unable or unwilling to remain or return.

The U.N. High Commissioner for Refugees (UNHCR) has defined "temporary protection" of refugees as "a means, in situations of large-scale influx and in view of the impracticality of conducting individual refugee status determination procedures, for providing protection to groups or categories of persons who are in need of international protection." Temporary protection "is primarily conceived as an emergency protection measure of short duration in response to large-scale influxes, guaranteeing admission to safety, protection from non-refoulement and respect for an appropriate standard of treatment." The first time the UNHCR formally recommended the granting of temporary protection involved "persons fleeing the conflict and human rights abuses in the former Yugoslavia."

The principle of international law called non-refoulement is the prohibition of forced return. This means a country has a duty not to return an individual to a country where he or she will face persecution. Article 33(1) of the Refugee Convention provides, "No Contracting State shall expel or return ('refouler') a refugee in any manner whatsoever to the frontiers of territories where his life or freedom would be threatened on account of his race, religion, nationality, membership of a particular social group or political opinion." Even if a country is not a party to the Refugee Convention, it is bound by the customary international law norm of non-refoulement.

As reported in a recent *New York Times* editorial, immigrants provide many more benefits than burdens, including paying more in taxes than they claim in government benefits and doing jobs that are hard to fill. As the Congressional Budget Office concluded in 2013, gross domestic product would rise by 5.4 percent and the federal budget deficit would fall by $897 billion over the next

20 years if undocumented workers are given a path to citizenship and more work-based visas are made available to foreigners.

In accordance with its legal and moral duty, the United States should step up to the plate and welcome significant numbers of refugees. More than 20 former senior Democratic and Republican officials are urging the Obama administration to accept 100,000 Syrian refugees, and to contribute up to $2 billion to finance their resettlement and help international refugee efforts. The United States has already accepted 1,500 Syrian refugees since the beginning of the hostilities and has contributed more than $4 billion in humanitarian aid for them.

Instead of demanding regime change in Syria, the United States and its allies must stop providing weapons, training and funding to the violent opposition forces. They should enlist Russia and Iran in pursuing a diplomatic solution to this tragic conflict.

Up to this point, some of Syria's immediate neighbors—Turkey, Jordan, Iraq, Lebanon and Egypt—have taken in 95 percent of the refugees, according to Amnesty International. Turkey has accepted nearly 2 million, followed by Lebanon, which has taken over 600,000. Jordan has taken half a million. Iraq has accepted almost 250,000. Egypt has accepted more than 130,000.

Germany agreed to take 800,000 refugees. Britain will take in 20,000 Syrian refugees by 2020, at the rate of 4,000 per year. Canada will take 10,000; Australia will take 12,000 Syrian and Iraqi refugees; Venezuela will take 20,000.

But Saudi Arabia, the United Arab Emirates, Qatar, Oman, Bahrain and Kuwait—the wealthiest nations in the region—have taken none of the refugees. Likewise, Iran and Russia, which support the Assad government, have refused permanent residency or asylum to the refugees.

Some of the Syrian refugees are Palestinians who first became refugees after the 1947-48 Nakba, when 80 percent of historic Palestine was ethnically cleansed to create Israel. They are "double refugees." But Israel has refused to take in any Syrian refugees.

Israel has apparently forgotten that in 1939, 937 Jewish refugees seeking to escape the Nazis made the perilous ocean voyage on the SS *St. Louis*, but the United States turned them away. Forced to return to Europe, hundreds of them were then killed by Hitler's forces. The nations of the world, and particularly the United States, must ensure the current refugees obtain the shelter to which they are entitled.

No Easy Answers

Natalia Banulescu-Bogdan and Susan Fratzke

In the following viewpoint, Natalia Banulescu-Bogdan and Susan Fratzke explore the problems in Europe caused by the influx of refugees. They suggest that the issues are complex and must be understood before solutions can be found. They warn that the current crisis may become a normal situation, as countries and organizations have failed to find successful solutions. They suggest that a more comprehensive and sustainable response is needed. Natalia Banulescu-Bogdan and Susan Fratzke work for the Migration Policy Institute, a US nonprofit that studies the movement of people worldwide.

As you read, consider the following questions:

1. What percentage of immigrants arriving at European borders will qualify for refugee status or other protection?
2. What is the primary route of migrants and refugees into Europe?
3. What percentage of refugees and migrants arriving in Europe are male?

More than 487,000 people have arrived at Europe's Mediterranean shores in the first nine months of 2015, double all of 2014 and the highest number since record keeping began. The journey is fraught with danger—nearly 3,000 people

"Europe's Migration Crisis in Context: Why Now and What Next?" by Natalia Banulescu-Bogdan and Susan Fratzke, Migration Information Source (the online journal of the Migration Policy Institute), September 24, 2015, http://www.migrationpolicy.org/article/europe-migration-crisis-context-why-now-and-what-next. Reprinted by permission.

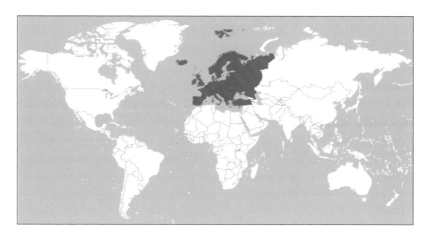

have perished crossing the Mediterranean this year alone, not counting those who lost their lives en route—and for those who do make it, their future in Europe remains highly uncertain.

With the unprecedented volumes of new arrivals, even the best-prepared European countries have reached a breaking point in their ability to meet European Union (EU) standards for receiving and processing applicants. Those with less experience managing immigration or hosting asylum seekers have given in at times to rash or counterproductive impulses. The question of who is responsible for those arriving has reignited deep internal divisions between Member States. Months of tense negotiations over efforts to relocate tens of thousands of asylum seekers from Greece and Italy resulted in a September 22 majority vote among EU interior ministers approving the relocation of 120,000 refugees across the continent, overriding objections to the redistribution scheme from several Eastern Member States. Frontline states such as Greece and Italy bear a disproportionate responsibility for receiving new arrivals, although most newcomers quickly move on to wealthier European Union (EU) countries including Sweden and Germany—which in 2015 received almost half of all EU asylum applications. In the process, a new front line has emerged in transit countries such as Hungary and Croatia that suddenly face enormous pressures at their borders, and in the case of Hungary the reaction has been to erect barbed-wire fencing and try at times to contain (or push back) the asylum seekers.

The flows themselves are extremely complex and driven by a complicated mix of factors. Although the majority of those arriving have protection needs (approximately three-quarters will qualify for refugee status or other protection), many are departing for Europe not from their countries of origin—where they face violence and persecution—but from places of first asylum, such as Turkey and Jordan, that have become overwhelmed by protection responsibilities. Globally, 86 percent of refugees are hosted in the developing world, which is rife with its own economic and political challenges. Ninety percent of the 4 million Syrians displaced outside their country's borders, for instance, are located in just three countries—Turkey, Jordan, and Lebanon. As the war continues into its fifth year and resources and opportunities in these countries dry up, more of the displaced have begun looking to Europe for shelter.

As the sense of chaos at Europe's borders escalates—with 4,000 arrivals per day on the Greek islands and tent camps erected almost overnight in German cities upending any remaining sense of order—European destination countries find themselves with no easy solutions. What is clear is that an effective response will need to be grounded in an understanding of the root causes of the flows, why they have spiked now, and what is likely to be the next pressure point. The costs of failure could be high. In the face of seemingly endless spontaneous arrivals, systems are caving under pressure, and trust and solidarity are eroding—between Member States, between publics and their governments, and within the global-protection system as a whole.

Shifting Routes: The Scale and Nature of the Challenge

The flow of migrants and refugees crossing the Mediterranean has increased dramatically, with the United Nations High Commissioner for Refugees (UNHCR) recording more than

487,000 arrivals by sea so far this year, up from 23,000 three years ago. In August alone, there were more than 130,000 maritime arrivals—a near quadrupling of the number seen in August 2014.

Migrants and refugees arrive via three primary routes, the relative significance of which has shifted throughout 2015:

- Central Mediterranean Route (Italy and Malta): More than 120,000 migrants and refugees arrived in Europe via the Central Mediterranean between January and September. Most have traveled on smugglers' boats departing from Libya, Tunisia, or Egypt. This extremely dangerous route dominated flows during 2014 and was the location of large-scale tragedies in October 2013 and April 2015, prompting calls for an EU-level response. The Central Mediterranean has diminished in use in 2015, partly due to increased instability in Libya, but remains the primary entry point for sub-Saharan nationals with few alternative routes. Eritreans and Nigerians have been the largest groups traveling the Central Mediterranean in 2015.

- Eastern Mediterranean Route (Greece/Aegean Sea): The Eastern Mediterranean has become the primary maritime route in 2015. More than 350,000 individuals have crossed from Turkey to Greece (the vast majority to Greek islands like Lesbos and Kos near the Turkish coast) in the first nine months of 2015. The shift in flows to the Eastern Mediterranean has been primarily driven by a change in migration patterns among Syrians, who have found it easier and safer to travel to Europe via Turkey to Greece. The short journey from Turkey to the Greek islands, just a few miles away, is safer than the much longer Central Mediterranean route. There are some reports of refugees undertaking the journey themselves, without relying on smugglers. Afghan and Pakistani nationals also arrive via the Eastern Mediterranean.

- Western Balkans (Hungary): More than 155,000 people crossed from Serbia into Hungary between January and August. Two primary groups travel this route: Western Balkan nationals—especially from Kosovo and Albania— and migrants and refugees traveling onward from Greece to reach the rest of the European Union. As arrivals to Greece have increased, so too has traffic through the Balkans and across the Hungarian border.

The largest numbers come from Syria—accounting for more than 50 percent of arrivals in 2015—followed by Eritrea, Afghanistan, Kosovo, Nigeria, Iraq, and several West African states including Senegal, Gambia, and Mali. Of those submitting asylum claims, Syrians and Eritreans are the most likely to be granted protection (more than 90 percent of both groups receive refugee status or another form of protection). Afghans, Iraqis, and Somalis are also likely to be granted refugee protection, while fewer than 5 percent of claims from Western Balkan nationals are accepted.

Economic Migrant or Refugee?

All three routes receive mixed flows composed of three primary groups: 1) individuals whose protection claims are likely to be recognized by European authorities, such as Syrians and Eritreans; 2) individuals fleeing instability or violence in their home countries who may not qualify for refugee status but are still at risk for other reasons including Somalis and some Syrians; and 3) migrants who feel compelled to leave their countries for largely economic reasons—Western Balkans and sub-Saharan nationals, for example.

Despite the distinct legal categories into which new arrivals are slotted, individuals have complex and overlapping motivations for leaving their origin countries that defy simple categorization. Even for those fleeing conflict or oppressive regimes, it is often difficult to pinpoint one precipitating push factor, especially one that aligns with the legal grounds for claiming asylum. The 1951 Geneva Convention offers a single definition of a refugee: someone fleeing a well-founded fear of persecution due to race, religion, nationality, membership in a particular social group, or political opinion. Ultimately, opportunity differentials continue to drive most movements, even for refugees. For many, reaching Europe means the chance to build or regain a normal life that has been disrupted by political or economic turmoil, conflict, or persecution. Thus while international law draws a bright line between refugees and other migrants (requiring very different treatment for the former), this distinction is much more nuanced in practice.

Even the motivations of those seen as primarily "economic migrants" may not be completely clear. Western Balkan nationals, for example, face extremely high unemployment and poverty rates, and have a clear economic incentive to seek entry to Europe. Roma or other minority ethnic groups that face severe and systemic discrimination in their home countries and could, in some cases, be considered grounds for refugee status represent a substantial share of those making the journey.

Motivations to move may also shift as conflicts wear on. While more than 4 million Syrians have found safety in neighboring countries, these countries have yet to provide the full legal status or rights entitled to refugees under the 1951 Refugee Convention—including the all-important right to work. With few opportunities to resume a normal life or economic self-sufficiency in first-asylum countries, and little hope that conditions will improve in the future, many Syrians are choosing to search for their own solutions in Europe.

The diversity of these flows—both in terms of the nationalities of those arriving and the motivations of individuals themselves—creates an added challenge for asylum authorities trying to determine who is a "genuine" refugee, who may qualify for another form of protection, and who does not have legal grounds to stay in the European Union. Each arrival must receive an individual assessment of his or her claim for protection, often a lengthy and resource-intensive process, and backlogs of claims awaiting adjudication have begun to grow in many Member States as authorities lack the means to keep up with the rising number of cases. But even those whose claims are denied stand a chance of remaining in the European Union, as return rates for failed asylum seekers remain low.

Why Now?

The arrival of Syrian refugees in Europe is not a new phenomenon. The Syrian civil war erupted in March 2011, leading to a steady escalation in the number of Syrians seeking protection in Europe since. These arrivals had already revealed fissures in the Common European Asylum System (CEAS), which provides common standards governing processing and reception in each of the 28 EU Member States' national asylum systems. But the near-exponential surge in the spring and summer of 2015 has nearly brought the struggling CEAS to its knees, overwhelming the capacity of policymakers and publics to respond. Many onlookers were left asking: why now? This escalation can be attributed to a confluence of intersecting push-and-pull factors, some of which have been simmering for years (and have simply been exacerbated by the passage of time and/or recent triggering events), others of which are new.

The combination of push factors includes: (1) the ongoing violence and instability in origin countries that have both precipitated mass movements and made return impossible (at least in the short to medium term); (2) the deterioration of conditions in countries of first asylum which has led some, including Jordan and Lebanon, to tighten their borders, limiting access to nearby safe havens for the displaced; (3) the continued lack of opportunities to work or enroll in school for most refugees, which is a major driver of onward movements; and (4) geopolitical changes that have closed off alternative destinations, such as Libya.

While many of these conditions are not new, they have intensified over time. The longer people remain displaced, with little prospect of return, the greater the burden on host countries that are themselves facing enormous political and economic struggles. Turkey, for example, has spent more than US$6 billion hosting refugees. In Lebanon, where tensions have been particularly acute, Syrians now comprise close to one-quarter of the population and by some counts Syrian children exceed the entire capacity of Lebanon's public schools. More than half of Syrians in Lebanon and one-sixth of refugees in Jordan are living in extreme poverty. Services in host communities are inundated, and opportunities to access essentials like education or health care have become limited for refugee and host communities alike. And as times get tougher, public opinion can sour. Initial generosity toward short-term "guests" does not always translate to support for permanent neighbors, who may compete with natives for jobs and limited spots in schools.

Geopolitical and economic changes over the last several years have added to migration pressures in the region. The armed conflicts and political crises currently facing Libya and Egypt have led not only to the suspension of bilateral and EU migration-enforcement agreements with those countries, but disrupted regional labor markets and migration flows within northern Africa. Libya in particular was a regional hub for migrant labor before the Arab Spring. Estimates put the migrant worker population in the country in 2011 at close to 2.5 million, including many sub-Saharan nationals. Many migrants who returned to work in the country since the overthrow of the Gadhafi regime have become stranded in an increasingly unstable Libya and chosen to cross to Europe in an effort to escape the growing conflict.

On the other end of the spectrum, policy announcements by European governments, as well as the creative use of social media, may have created new enabling (or pull) factors. Some individuals who had previously resisted leaving may feel emboldened by news of their compatriots having successfully arrived in Europe alongside reports of countries like Germany or Sweden granting status to most Syrians who make it to their territory. Social media enables these "success" stories to spread instantaneously, along with tips on how to navigate the journey and access critical services upon

Businesses and Humanitarian Needs

The number of refugees and internally displaced people is at its highest since the Second World War. The structure and resources of the humanitarian system are increasingly insufficient to meet the needs of people fleeing conflict. Understanding that the primary responsibility for peace rests with Governments, the magnitude and urgency of current emergencies require support from all actors in society – including business.

The global refugee crisis unfolding across Europe, the Middle East and Africa challenges the world, but also presents an enormous opportunity for businesses to be a force for good. All aspects of the refugee crisis are better managed when different stakeholders come together to look for people-driven, values-based approaches where public policies are met by responsible business operations, new business models, investment, innovation and technology.

Recognizing that business expertise, resources and innovative approaches can be leveraged to address humanitarian needs, the UN Global Compact Business for Peace platform has embarked on a project to promote and inspire private sector engagement in humanitarian action.

In September 2015, the UN Global Compact, in partnership with The UN Refugee Agency (UNHCR), launched a Business Action Pledge in Response to the Refugee Crisis to encourage the private sector to support existing efforts and provide solutions to the widespread societal disruption.

The Pledge calls on companies with operations or supply chains in countries that are producing, transiting and receiving refugees to determine how to best support, based on their own assets and capabilities. Companies can demonstrate leadership by taking action – as an individual company or in partnership with others.

"Take action in response to the refugee crisis," by Ms. Tiina Mylly, United Nations.

arrival. New initiatives like the "Airbnb for refugees" in Germany and Austria—albeit small-scale—may make it easier for refugees who have fewer support systems or networks to navigate unfamiliar environments. In addition, the chaos at European borders means that even if individuals do not qualify for protection, there may be a long lag time before their claims are adjudicated, during which time many travel onward illegally through Europe. Finally, classic patterns of chain migration may also be responsible for some of the new flows, as settled migrants reunify with family and friends. And this may just be the tip of the iceberg. The refugees and migrants currently arriving on Europe's shores are almost 70 percent male, and media and nongovernmental organization (NGO) reports suggest that those arriving are "first movers" with family still abroad who intend to join them through legal channels once their claims are granted.

Why This Crisis Is So Difficult to Tackle

The sheer scale of displacement worldwide has tested the limits of the international protection regime built around the 1951 Refugee Convention and revealed existing fault lines and failures in current humanitarian policies. As of 2014, UNHCR estimates that 59.5 million people have been forcibly displaced from their homes, of whom 19.5 million are refugees outside their countries of origin. Three primary factors have limited the system's capacity to respond.

First, existing approaches to protection have proven singularly unable to find solutions for long-term displaced populations. Almost half of refugees under UNHCR's care in 2014 had been displaced for five years or more. For most, return to their origin country or resettlement in a third country remains a distant possibility; in 2014, approximately 105,000 refugees were resettled through UNHCR, representing less than 1 percent of all refugees displaced globally. Humanitarian responses in refugee situations have been criticized for focusing too heavily on the "care and maintenance" of refugee populations, leaving refugees essentially "warehoused" for years on end, their lives in limbo, with little focus on long-term, sustainable solutions.

Second, the international community has failed to offer anything like meaningful burden-sharing to host countries in conflict regions, which care for the vast majority of the world's refugees. Neither assistance funding nor resettlement places—

insufficient before the latest surge in displacement—have increased apace with the level of need. And the resources that are available are finite, and dwindle as time wears on. In Lebanon, for example, the World Food Program (WFP) announced in July it would have to reduce food vouchers given to Syrian refugees by half. The 2015 UN joint appeal for the region had received just 40 percent of requested funding as of September. Although all categories of the appeal are underfunded, support for livelihoods development and host-community resilience has been particularly low, adding to the prospect of long-term vulnerability in the affected countries. European leaders acknowledged the significance of the funding gap facing the Syria refugee response at an extraordinary EU summit on September 23, promising an additional 1 billion euros to UNHCR and WFP to ease the deficit (half will come from EU funds and half from Member States). Prior to the latest announcement, European countries had provided more than one-third of the funding for the United Nations' response, with the United States providing a further one-third of the financing. But outside Europe and the United States, financial support for the Syria region has been less than forthcoming. Other than Japan, no countries in Asia or Latin America have contributed, and while Kuwait has been the third largest financial contributor to the international response, other Gulf countries such as Saudi Arabia have come under criticism for not doing more.

Furthermore, UNHCR-reported resettlement departures have barely increased over 2009 levels. Countries not immediately affected by the crisis have been slow to offer resettlement places. Recent offers by traditional resettlement countries like Australia, Canada, and the United States to provide an additional 10,000-12,000 places each for Syrians are just a drop in the bucket in comparison with the 4 million refugees who have been displaced. And so far offers from countries without established resettlement programs have been even less forthcoming.

Finally, the principles of protection enshrined in the Refugee Convention (in particular the requirement that refugees be located outside their country of origin) have resulted in territorially based national asylum systems—refugees must gain access to a state's territory in order to exercise their rights to claim asylum. At the same time, wealthy nations have undertaken a large-scale effort to secure and "push out" their borders. Visa restrictions and airline sanctions, for example, have made it difficult—if not impossible—for most of those seeking protection to reach their destinations through common means of entry. As a result, refugees are forced to rely on increasingly risky and dangerous routes, often requiring the use of smugglers, to gain entry to asylum systems in Europe and elsewhere.

A Global Challenge

Although the absolute scale of protection needs facing Europe is still smaller than that in many countries of first asylum—though this is rapidly shifting—the unplanned, fast-changing, and unevenly distributed nature of the flows has caused serious difficulties for countries with highly organized immigration and integration systems, labor markets, and social services. Emerging struggles in many European countries to continue to provide for new arrivals at a high standard—the deteriorating conditions on the Greek islands are one highly visible example—raise the possibility that there may be a limit to what Europe can handle. Several international aid organizations, normally operating in countries like Iraq or Pakistan, have now launched assistance programming in Europe (for example, the International Rescue Committee, World Vision, Save the Children, and Doctors without Borders are all now operational in Europe).

Given that few truly innovative or large-scale solutions to the growing protection challenge have so far presented themselves, what is seen at Europe's borders may not be a "crisis" but rather the new normal.

Migration flows are inherently difficult to predict, but none of the push factors driving refugees and migrants to Europe's shores appear likely to be resolved soon. Little progress has so far been made in resolving the political situation in Syria, suggesting ISIS and other extremist groups will have plenty of room to continue exploiting the power vacuum in large parts of the country. Related violence in neighboring Iraq is likely to add to the refugee flows.

Meanwhile, patience and capacity in neighboring countries are clearly wearing thin. Jordan, Turkey, and Lebanon, for example, while generously opening their doors to millions of Syrians, have strongly resisted granting refugees formal legal status or rights that would encourage their long-term integration, instead referring to them as "guests." As a result, refugees' rights and opportunities in these countries remain limited. Both Lebanon and Jordan have also restricted access to their territory for Syrians, driving new flows to Turkey where authorities have turned a blind eye to smugglers moving people on to Europe. In the absence of a large-scale increase in support for these countries (both in terms of aid and resettlement), it should come as a shock to no one that refugees continue to seek more stable conditions and longer-term solutions in Europe's asylum systems.

Elsewhere, conflict and oppression seem unlikely to abate. Political oppression in Eritrea, including forced conscription, will continue to drive flows. At the same time, growing instability in Egypt and escalating conflicts in Libya and Yemen may prove to be new sources for refugee flows to Europe; violence in Yemen has already driven many to seek safety across the Gulf of Aden in Somalia—reversing long-time regional flows. Yet Europe has few early-warning systems in place equipped to predict mass movements before they happen. Indeed, migration is usually used as an indicator of brewing political conflicts or large-scale natural disasters, rather than a policy target in and of itself. In the short term, the usual reduction in Mediterranean arrivals over the winter months may not materialize as migrants and refugees use the shorter and safer crossing from Turkey to Greece.

Against this new landscape, countries in Europe and elsewhere will have to think hard about how to approach their protection responsibilities. Giving in to the impulses to erect bigger fences without concomitantly dealing with the root causes of these movements will only serve to deepen the pockets of smugglers, not reduce the flows themselves. Most thinking has pointed to a need to approach refugee- and migrant-producing situations in a much more comprehensive way that moves beyond humanitarian and asylum tools alone. In a more connected and mobile world, waiting to deal with a problem until it reaches a country's borders is not sustainable. In the same vein, providing protection can no longer be seen as a purely national responsibility; responses that mobilize both financial and political resources at the regional—and global—levels will need to become the new normal.

Sources

Economist, The. 2015. How many migrants to Europe are refugees?" The Economist, September 7, 2015. Available Online.

European Asylum Support Office (EASO). 2015. Annual Report on the Situation of Asylum in the European Union 2014. Luxembourg: EASO. Available Online.

Eurostat. 2015. Asylum in the EU: Over 210,000 first time asylum seekers in the EU in the second quarter of 2015. News release, September 18, 2015. Available Online.

Frontex. 2015. Annual Risk Analysis 2015. Warsaw: Frontex. Available Online.

———. 2015. Migratory Routes Map. Accessed September 23, 2015. Available Online.

Guild, Elspeth and Karin Zwaan. 2014. Does Europe Still Create Refugees? Examining the Situation of the Roma. Queen's Law Journal 40 (1).

Hurriyet Daily News. 2015. Turkey urges world's help on Syrian refugees as spending reaches $6 billion. Hurriyet Daily News, February 27, 2015. Available Online.

Migration Policy Centre (MPC). 2013. Libya: Migration Profile. Florence: MPC. Available Online.

United Nations High Commissioner for Refugees (UNHCR). 2015. Global Trends 2014: World at War. Geneva: UNHCR. Available Online.

————. 2015. Refugees endure worsening conditions as Syria's conflict enters 5th year. Press release, March 12, 2015. Available Online.

————. 2015. Refugees/Migrants Emergency Response – Mediterranean. Accessed September 24, 2015. Available Online.

————. 2015. Syria Regional Response Portal. Accessed September 22, 2015. Available Online.

UNHCR and United Nations Development Program (UNDP). 2015. 3RP Regional Refugee & Resilience Plan: Funding Snapshot – Top Donor Group Meeting, September 2015. Amman: UNHCR and UNDP. Available Online.

United Nations Office for the Coordination of Humanitarian Affairs (UNOCHA), Financial Tracking Service. 2015. Total Funding to the Syrian Crisis 2015. Accessed September 22, 2015. Available Online.

Wall, Indonesia. 2015. Response or opportunism? IRIN News, September 15, 2015. Available Online.

World Food Program (WFP). 2015. Vulnerability Assessment of Syrian Refugees (VASyR): Preliminary Results. Rome: WFP. Available Online.

Find Work for Refugees

Paul Collier

In the following viewpoint, Paul Collier suggests that the answer to the refugee crisis is not about Europe taking in more refugees. Rather, it should mean helping people return to their country of origin. This would involve giving Syrians in exile temporary work in neighboring countries, until the violence in Syria abates and they can return home. He suggests that businesses as well as governments could help make this happen. Paul Collier is a British economist and author.

As you read, consider the following questions:

1. What percentage of Syria's population is now displaced?
2. Of these, how many remain in Syria?
3. How do Syrians in Jordan lacks autonomy?

For all its difficulties, Europe is prosperous and safe: one of the best places on Earth. Many other societies have yet to achieve this happy state: some are murderous and poor. Two of the most troubled zones in the world are near Europe: the Middle East, and the Sahelian belt which spans northern Africa.

Unsurprisingly, many of the people who live in these societies would rather live in Europe. Impeded by immigration controls, a small minority of this group are taking matters into their own hands, trying to enter Europe illegally by boat across the Mediterranean. Some succeed, like those now camped in Calais, trying to smuggle their way on to trains and trucks bound for Britain. Others board boats that sink, leaving them floundering in the Med. Sporadically, official Europe rescues these people in a fit of conscience. As with the euro itself, high principle has collided with low politics and the result is avoidable suffering.

Unlike the euro, it would not be difficult to put right. If you step outside the usual angry ding-dong, the posturing of those both pro-immigrant and anti-immigrant; if you resist the easy option taken by the chattering classes who claim the moral high ground by insisting on open borders, you can see that European policy is the result of moral confusion.

Let's take the 'duty of rescue', which is official Europe's rationale for fishing people out of the sea. People have a right to dream of a life in Europe, but Europe has a moral obligation to rescue, not to make dreams come true.

What does rescue imply and to whom does it apply? Just being poor does not make someone eligible for being 'rescued' by a life in Europe. Mass poverty has to be tackled, but the only way it can be done is for poor countries to catch up with the rich ones. There are ways in which we can help that process, but encouraging the mass emigration of their most enterprising young people is not one of them. What makes people truly entitled to rescue is if their ordinary lives are made impossible by violent conflict — and in the current crisis, that means focusing on Syria. Yes, there are other legitimate refugees on those boats, but Syrians alone account for around 40 per cent of the boat people crossing the Mediterranean.

And those Syrians waving and drowning in the sea are merely the tip of a vastly larger iceberg of need. Of Syria's 20 million people, around half are now displaced. This ten million are the submerged iceberg: the group to whom we have some duty of rescue. They are displaced through circumstance rather than choice. The tiny minority (about 2 per cent) in the sea and camped on our doorstep are part of our duty of rescue, but they should not be allowed to crowd out the needs of others: for one thing, they tend to be richer and more resourceful.

Of the ten million who are displaced, around half are still in Syria, trapped now that Jordan and Lebanon have closed their borders. It is obviously more difficult for Europe to help the internally displaced within Syria, but there are still ways of doing so. These five million should not be forgotten just because they have not created a problem for other nations.

The other five million are in neighbouring countries: mostly in Jordan, Lebanon and Turkey. How can Europe help these people? The official international solution to refugee situations is camps, a strategy dating back to 1947. This system is not working and, indeed, it cannot possibly work. Just look at Jordan. Nearly 90 per cent of the refugees in Jordan have chosen not to live in the camps but have instead drifted to the cities. They forgo handouts in favour of scratching a living in illegal employment.

So what is wrong with the camps? Having recently visited the largest, Za'atari, I doubt whether it is the standard of living. The UNHCR does a commendable job: people are well-fed and their housing conditions are far superior to the African cities with which I am more familiar. Whatever our duty of rescue to Syrian refugees, improving the material conditions of the camps is not a priority. The problem of the camps is that people have no autonomy: most especially, they are not allowed to work.

In a jobless Arab household in the camps, it is hard for parents to retain authority. Teenage girls are lured into prostitution, teenage boys drift back to Syria and to armed gangs. The lack of autonomy extends beyond work: although there are around 200 Syrian teachers living as refugees in camps, they live in enforced idleness. Refugee children are taught by Jordanian teachers to the Jordanian curriculum. It's not surprising that refugees overwhelmingly prefer penurious freedom to the restrictions of the camps.

Why is autonomy in the cities penurious? Because the Jordanian authorities do not let refugees work. Given the scale of the influx, the Jordanians are unsurprisingly worried that letting the Syrians work could destabilise their society and, given the disorder elsewhere in the Middle East, this cannot be lightly dismissed. Jordanian security depends upon a complex and delicate system of political inclusion which links the monarchy organically and historically to each part of society. Syrians cannot readily be inserted into this system, which means a section of future Jordanian society will be disconnected and thereby disaffected.

If the Jordanian authorities will not integrate refugees into their society, what can Europe do for them? Should we invite them to Europe? This has been the defining issue so far in European discussion of the Syrian refugee crisis: 'How many refugees should Europe take?' It's all about us. Unfortunately, while well meaning, this approach is fundamentally irresponsible when judged from the perspective not of the consequences for Europe, but the consequences for Syrians.

Our duty is to provide better futures for as many of the displaced as possible — and their overwhelming hope is not to live permanently in Europe, but to return to a post-conflict Syria. Effective rescue should be about salvaging as much of their disrupted lives as possible. Of course, if they are in the sea, rescue involves pulling them out of it. But any action needs to be set within a larger strategy of making people's return viable.

The key fact to grasp about the Syrian conflict is that it will end; conflicts in middle–income countries seldom last more than a decade and this one has already been running for four years. There is an obvious endgame, in which the Syrian army dumps Assad as a liability and leads a broad anti-Isis alliance. Once parts of Syria return to peace, they will face a fairly standard challenge of post-conflict recovery. Post-conflict situations are politically fragile, and rapid economic recovery helps to stabilise them. The smart way to meet the duty to rescue is to incubate that economic recovery now, before the conflict ends.

Europe can do that by fostering a Syria–in-exile economy located in Jordan and other neighbouring countries. Working in this economy would restore some dignity to the daily lives of refugees and offer them credible hope of a return to normality. Providing a skilled minority of Syrians with dream lives in Europe is not the answer: it would be detrimental to recovery because once settled in Europe, with their children in schooling, such people would be unlikely to go back to a post-conflict society. In consequence, it would gut Syria of the very people it will most need. It is an intellectually lazy feel-good policy for the bien-pensant.

Just minutes from the Za'atari camp is an empty industrial zone, fully equipped with infrastructure. This could be a perfect haven of employment, the means by which Europe could incubate Syrian post-conflict recovery. This zone alone is large enough to employ the labour force of Za'atari several times over. The people working there would recover their autonomy, and have a prospect of relocating to Syria when the war is over. The zone could house Syrian businesses that cannot continue to function at home, as well as a cluster of global companies producing for the European market. It could employ both Syrians and Jordanians. Europe could provide the incentives which make this happen. Each job created could attract a subsidy financed out of the money Europe quite rightly earmarks for assistance to fragile states, and their work could be given open access to European markets.

Once peace returns, these businesses could relocate with their returning Syrian workforce, while also continuing to operate in Jordan with their Jordanian workforce. The Jordanian authorities would be supportive because it offers a credible alternative to the permanent settlement which they fear, and would attract global firms to Jordan. The approach could be replicated with Syria's other neighbours.

Job havens would not only assist refugees; indirectly they would help the five million displaced who remain in Syria. In return for European assistance, the neighbouring governments could be asked to re-open their borders. Accessible and attractive safe havens across the border would be a lifeline for these internally displaced people. As firms and workers relocated to the havens, it would put further financial pressure on Assad.

Victorian ladies would sometimes deliberately leave valuables conspicuously 'mislaid' in the hopes that their servants would succumb to stealing them, affording their mistresses delectable opportunities for moral grandstanding. We now recognise this as a breach of a basic moral duty of the fortunate towards the less fortunate: 'Thou shall not tempt.' Currently, if a refugee can get a foot on a European beach, or be fished out of the sea by a European rescue vessel, they get privileged access to asylum. That is why they take the risk.

This legal structure is not just foolish, it is deeply immoral. Europe has a duty to fish refugees out of the sea because it is morally responsible for tempting them on to the sea. So whatever else Europe does, it must stop this policy of temptation. Paying a crook thousands of dollars for a place on a boat should not entitle a Syrian refugee to a more privileged entry to Europe. It is profoundly unfair to the other suffering refugees.

Periodical and Internet Sources Bibliography

The following articles have been selected to supplement the diverse views presented in this chapter.

Agenda for Humanity, World Humanitarian Summit. http://www. worldhumanitariansummit.org/

Priscilla Alvarez, "What Should the US Do about Refugee Settlement?" The Atlantic, March 29, 2016.

http://www.theatlantic.com/politics/archive/2016/03/refugee-resettlement-united-states/474939/

Scott Arbeiter, "Americas Duty to Take in Refugees," The New York Times, September 23, 2016. www.nytimes.com/2016/09/24/opinion/americas-duty-to-take-in-refugees.html

Ban Ki-moon, UN Secretary-General, "In Safety and Dignity: Addressing Large Movements of Refugees and Migrants", United Nations, April 21, 2016. http://www.un.org/pga/70/wp-content/uploads/sites/10/2015/08/21-Apr_Refugees-and-Migrants-21-April-2016.pdf

European Commission, "Balancing Responsibility and Solidarity on Migration and Asylum", European Commission, 2016. https://ec.europa.eu/home-affairs/sites/homeaffairs/files/what-we-do/policies/european-agenda-migration/background-information/docs/balancing_responsibility_and_solidarity_on_migration_and_asylum_20160210_en.pdf

Damian Grammaticas, "Europe's Migrant Crisis: Tricky Business to Resolve", BBC News. March 8, 2016. http://www.bbc.com/news/world-europe-35760115

"How Is the Migrant Crisis Dividing EU Countries?" BBC News. March 4, 2016. http://www.bbc.com/news/world-europe-34278886

JepH Juergens, "Syrian Refugees Are An American Problem (Because Guess Who Caused All This)", Thought Catalog, February 23, 2016.

http://thoughtcatalog.com/jeph-juergens/2016/02/syrian-refugees-are-an-american-problem/

Gavin Lee, "Desperate Migrants Plead to Escape 'Hellish' Greek Camp", BBC News, March 2, 2016. http://www.bbc.com/news/world-europe-35707452

Mark Urban, "Europe's Migrant Story Enters New Phase", BBC News, May 10, 2016. http://www.bbc.com/news/world-europe-36246816

"Why Is EU Struggling with Migrants and Asylum?" BBC News, March 3, 2016. http://www.bbc.com/news/world-europe-24583286

GLOBALVIEWPOINTS

CHAPTER 3

The Benefits and Dangers of Immigration

More Immigration Will Be Good for the US Economy

Giovanni Peri

In the following viewpoint, Giovanni Peri notes that the United States is a magnet for immigrants. Many more people would like to immigrate, including skilled workers. He believes that if the US increases its number of immigrants, companies will invest to create more jobs, so the greater number of workers will not hurt wages. He believes that a reform bill allowing for more immigration to the US would be good for the economy. Giovanni Peri is chair of the department of economics at the University of California-Davis.

As you read, consider the following questions:

1. How many immigrants are now in the United States?
2. What age group is most likely to immigrate?
3. What two groups are most likely to immigrate, in terms of education levels?

Immigration has always been a formidable engine of economic and demographic growth for the United States. During the last decades of the 19th century, immigrants contributed substantially, providing labor for the industrialization and electrification of the country. That wave of immigration was ended by the very restrictive immigration laws passed in 1929. While the "Immigration and Nationality Act" of 1965 abolished national quotas and allowed

"The Economic Benefits of Immigration", by Giovanni Peri, The Regents of the University of California, August 13, 2015. Reprinted by permission.

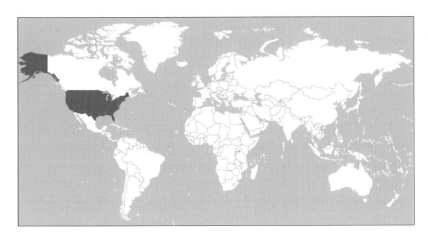

the flow of immigrants to resume, it has only been during the last 30 years that the mobility of the world's people has increased significantly. Young, motivated, and often highly educated people are on the move, and many of them would like to come to the United States. With its 41 million immigrants, the United States is by far the largest magnet for international migrants. Moreover, according to Gallup World Polls, there are about 150 million more people who say that they would migrate to the United States (from every country on the planet) if they had the opportunity.

While immigration flows, if managed efficiently and flexibly, would bring strong opportunities for economic growth, U.S. immigration laws remain outdated, cumbersome, and rather restrictive. These laws have substantially limited immigration for work-related reasons, both among the highly educated (scientists and engineers) and the less educated (construction, agricultural, and personal service workers). The misalignment between restrictive laws and economic incentives has also caused the population of undocumented immigrants to expand rapidly. Attracted by employment, but unable to secure a legal permit, 11 million people work and have set down roots in the United States, despite great uncertainty and little protection.

On June 27, 2013, the U.S. Senate seemed set to change all that, by passing Senate Bill 744, the "Border Security, Economic

Opportunity, and Immigration Modernization Act." The bill is the result of compromise, and is therefore imperfect. Still, it could become the most important piece of legislation on immigration of the last 50 years. It addresses most of the relevant issues plaguing the U.S. immigration system and deals with the problem of undocumented immigrants. As of today, however, due to political polarization, it seems unlikely that the House will pass the bill, despite its potential benefits for the U.S. economy.

Who Migrates to the U.S. for Economic Reasons?

Abundant research, based on comprehensive data on net migration to rich countries, has shown that two groups have a much higher propensity to migrate internationally. The first group consists of the highly educated, in particular, college-educated individuals. They have emigration rates four to five times higher than workers with no college education, and in poor countries, they are 10 to 12 times more likely to migrate. The second group is made up of the young: individuals between 20 and 40 years of age have the highest propensity to migrate. After 45, few people choose to leave their home countries.

Looking at the United States, a very large group of immigrants (as a percentage of the native population with similar skills) is made up of young, highly educated workers, mainly scientists and engineers. Another large group consists of young workers with little education who are employed in highly manual-intensive occupations. Figure 1 shows that ordering schooling levels from low to high and reporting the percentage of foreign-born workers for each skill group reveals a clear, U-shaped distribution. The percentage of foreign-born workers, as of 2011, was very high among workers with no degree, mainly employed in manual-intensive jobs. It was also very high among highly educated science, technology, engineering, and math workers (STEM). The percentage of foreign-born workers was much smaller for intermediate levels of education. The group of immigrants with very little education included a large part of the undocumented workers. This was due, in part, to the fact that there are very few legal ways for foreign workers with low schooling levels to enter the United States, despite there being significant demand for them. The current composition of U.S. immigrants follows the labor market logic. Adapting immigration laws to reflect this logic, as the proposed reform would do, makes perfect sense and would improve efficiency.

The Economic Effects of Immigrants

The very simple logic of demand and supply implies that, other thing being fixed, an increase in the labor supply reduces wages as workers compete in an increasingly crowded economy. While correct on its face, this is "partial equilibrium" reasoning. Since partial equilibrium models rely on the assumption that other things are kept fixed, they do not account for the series of adjustments and responses of the economy to immigration. Still, that simple logic is often pushed to its Malthusian implication that more workers in an economy mean lower wages and lower incomes. These partial equilibrium implications are likely to be incorrect, theoretically and empirically, in "general equilibrium." The workings of four important mechanisms attenuate — and often reverse — the partial effects of an increased supply of foreign workers on the demand for native workers.

Investments

First, as a consequence of the availability of more workers, firms invest: they expand their productive capacity and build more establishments. The productive capacity (capital) per worker has grown in the U.S. economy at a constant rate during the period from 1960 to 2009. If anything, capital per worker was higher when immigration was at its peak in 2007 than it was in 1990 before the immigration boom began. Investments, that is, were responsive to the predictable inflows of workers. Hence, immigrants did not crowd out existing firms over the long run. Rather, they increased the size and number of firms providing investment opportunities.

Educational Composition of Immigrants

Second, workers are not all the same. In terms of their labor market skills, there is a large difference between workers with tertiary education and those with a secondary education or less. It makes sense to distinguish between these two groups because they do different jobs. A modified version of the wage-depressing effect of immigrants is that, if the relative supply of less-educated workers among the foreign-born is larger, their inflow would depress the wages of less-educated natives relative to highly educated natives. In the U.S., however, because of the combination of immigrants at the top and the bottom of the schooling distribution (as seen in the chart below), immigrants have had a balanced distribution. The overall proportion of college-educated immigrants has been very similar to that of natives. So, their inflow did not significantly alter the relative supply of those two broad groups. Labor economists consider the split between the tertiary and non-tertiary educated as the most relevant factor for understanding the effects of relative supply on relative wages. Since immigration did not alter the relative supply of these two groups, it is unlikely to have changed their relative wages. At the national level, immigration cannot explain the observed increase in the relative wage of college-educated workers versus high-school graduates observed in the 1980s and 1990s, simply because it did not much affect that relative supply.

Specialization and Technology: Job Upgrades

It is even more interesting to consider the differentiation of skills and productive characteristics between natives and immigrants within each of the two education groups. One tendency among immigrant workers with little schooling is to concentrate predominately in manual jobs. They tend to work as farm laborers, construction workers, roofers, drivers, food preparers, housekeepers, and caregivers for children and the elderly. Similarly educated natives, on the other hand, tend to work in jobs that require more intensive communication and interaction skills; they are cooks, construction supervisors, farm coordinators, and clerks.

Percentage of foreign-born US workers, by educational attainment, 2014

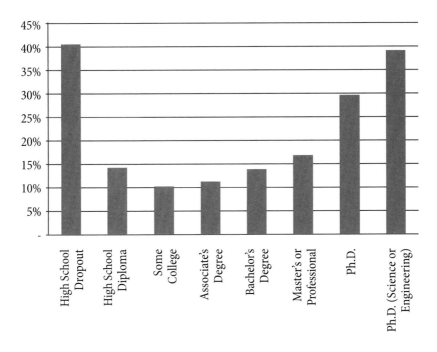

In a study I conducted with Chad Sparber ("Task Specialization, Immigration and Wages," American Economic Journal: Applied Economics, 1:3, July, 2009), we show that, due to the limited knowledge of the language, immigrants specialize in manual jobs. As a consequence, firms and sectors that hire immigrants generate higher demand for jobs requiring coordination, communication, and interaction — jobs that are typically staffed by natives, whose language skills are superior. This dynamic specialization according to skills pushes natives to upgrade their jobs to better paid, communication-intensive occupations and protects their wages from competition from immigrants. By taking the manual jobs that natives progressively leave, immigrants push a reorganization of production along specialization lines that may increase the effectiveness and efficiency of labor. A related line of research by Ethan Lewis at Dartmouth shows that, in markets with many immigrant workers, firms adopt techniques that are particularly efficient in the use of less- educated, manual-intensive workers. Hence, they are able to absorb a large number of less-educated manual workers without a loss in productivity and wages.

Mobility of Immigrants

Finally, immigrant workers, both newcomers and those already working in the United States, are more willing than natives to move in order to find jobs. Immigration, as a consequence, has served to smooth out local booms and busts; by moving away from declining regions and into booming areas, immigrants help stabilize the economy and reduce the "mismatch" between local demand for labor and its supply. Immigrants' willingness to move helps slow wage decline in stagnant regions and contributes to economic growth in booming ones. Combined with the complementarity of immigrants to natives, this mobility helps reinforce productivity growth in strong labor markets.

In summary, investment, the specialization of natives, the complementarity between natives and immigrants, and the technological response of firms are the local economy's margins of response to immigration. They all attenuate and may overturn the depressing effect of increased labor supply. These factors explain why a long line of empirical economic studies (first summarized by Friedberg and Hunt in 1995, and then by Longhi et al. in 2005) has found that immigration has, at most, a very small effect on native wages and employment at both the local and the national level. My recent studies on U.S. employment and wages (in particular "Rethinking the Effect of Immigration on Wages," Journal of the European Economic Association, John Wiley & Sons, Ltd., vol. 10(1), written with Gianmarco Ottaviano), found very small — a few fractions of a percentage point — positive effects of immigration on the wages of less-educated natives. Only a few studies (e.g., Borjas 2003, 2006) have found negative wage effects on less-educated workers at the national level. These effects amounted to a roughly 3 percent decline over the period from

1980 to 2000. Even those studies, however, found positive wage effects of 1 to 1.5 percent for workers with an intermediate to high schooling level.

Other Economic Effects of Immigrants

In the United States — and in many European countries — the foreign born have become a large and growing presence in the home services sector. Home services include cleaning, food preparation, and gardening, as well as personal services such as child and elderly care. These jobs are often characterized as "household production" services. The increased presence of immigrants in this sector has made home services more affordable, which in turn has allowed more native-born women — especially highly educated women — to join the labor force or to increase their hours worked. A study by Patricia Cortes at Boston University shows that the inflow of less-educated immigrants reduced the cost of household production services by almost 10 percent over the period from 1980 to 2000. Moreover, native women increased their work week by about half an hour because of less-expensive home-care services. Low-skilled immigrants thus allowed the productive potential of highly educated women to be used in the labor market by performing some of their household production tasks.

Highly Educated Immigrants: Contribution to Innovation

Highly educated immigrants are a huge asset for the U.S. economy, which attracts scientists and engineers from all over the world. One-quarter of the U.S.-based Nobel laureates of the last 50 years were foreign-born, and highly educated immigrants account for about one-third of U.S. innovation. In 2006, immigrants founded 25 percent of new high-tech companies with more than $1 million in sales, generating income and employment for the whole country. Innovation and technological growth are the engines of economic growth in technologically advanced countries like the United States, where attracting and training new scientists and engineers is key to continued economic success. In a recent paper I wrote with Chad Sparber and Kevin Shih, we show that the inflow of STEM workers driven by H-1B visas during the period 1990-2010 explains up to 30 percent of the productivity growth in U.S. cities. This growth has increased per capita income in the United States by 8 percent over the last 20 years.

Immigration Reforms

In light of these findings, I would like to emphasize that the Senate's reform proposal would constitute a strong economic stimulus for the U.S. economy. First, the bill increases the quota for H-1B (highly skilled) temporary visas, from 65,000 to 110,000 a year, and it allows the quota to grow up to 180,000. If current and past experience is any guide, most H-1B visas will go to scientists and engineers working in fast-growing sectors of the economy. Their innovations, entrepreneurship, and discoveries will be a powerful engine of economic productivity and wage growth.

Second, the reform introduces temporary visas for less-educated workers as well. The initial quota for these W visas is 20,000, and it can be increased up to 200,000 after four years, if demand from employers is sufficiently high. W visas are meant to ensure an adequate workforce in sectors where many jobs don't require a college degree. In recent decades, the high demand for these services and the pressure to keep their cost low have generated incentives to hire undocumented workers. The reform creates a legal channel for employers to fill these jobs at competitive wages after they've been advertised to native workers.

The long-run demographic and educational trends in the United States suggest that there will be a decreasing supply of natives for these occupations because the population is aging and becoming more educated. By hiring immigrants for manual jobs, companies create new jobs for natives as production expands overall and complementary workers are needed.

Finally, the bill envisions a path to permanent residence for 11 million immigrants who are without proper documents.

While the path is long and demanding, it sets the right economic incentives for the undocumented to continue working and contributing to the U.S. economy. First, it will allow workers to be more mobile and to find jobs that best match their abilities, likely increasing their productivity and wages in the short and medium run. Most studies identify wage gains of between 5 and 15 percent from acquiring legal status. Second, legal status will provide immigrants with incentives to invest in human capital and training. Young individuals will be more willing to get an education, which will further increase their productivity and wages. Older individuals will be more willing to train and acquire U.S.-specific skills, such as better language skills. Third, as the undocumented become more productive, their tax-paying ability will also grow. The Congressional Budget Office calculated that the increase in wages associated with legal status would generate a net increase in government revenues.

If Congress can set political bickering aside and pass this reform, certainly the U.S. economy would benefit, its citizens would be better off, and the country's immigration system would finally be ready to meet the needs of the 21st century.

Refugees Will Benefit Germany, If They Have Support

Victoria Rietig

In the following viewpoint, Victoria Rietig explores how refugees affect the German labor market. She references studies and opinions that say the impact will be positive, and others that predict negative consequences. Rietig notes that this is because studies use different assumptions. She lists five factors that affect how well immigrants adapt to life in Germany, with suggestions for improvements. Victoria Rietig is an expert consultant on migration and refugee issues.

As you read, consider the following questions:

1. How many immigrants entered Germany in 2015?
2. What are the five factors that affect how well immigrants adapt to the German workforce?
3. How long do asylum-seekers in Germany have to wait before they can enter the labor market?

G ermany is in the midst of a heated discussion: Are refugees a burden or a blessing for the German labor market?

Supporters of the "blessing" camp argue the country's aging society is in urgent need of young workers to make up for millions of retiring Germans. Around one third of the 1 million migrants and refugees who entered Germany in 2015 are under the age of

"Burden or Blessing? The Impact of Refugees on Germany's Labor Market," by Victoria Rietig. The American Institute for Contemporary German Studies, April 12, 2016, and available at www.aicgs.org. Reprinted by permission.

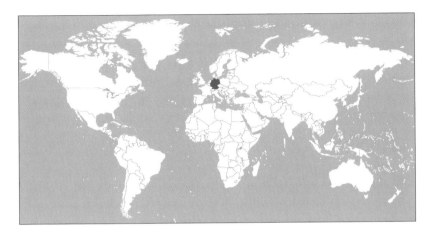

25[1] and their labor will help maintain the generous pension and benefits system Germans hold dear. The integration of refugees, the argument goes, may be costly for Germany in the short run, but refugees' contributions will outweigh these start-up costs after a few years, leaving the German economy better off.

In line with this thinking, a recent study of the German Institute for Economic Research (DIW), a think tank in Berlin, finds that the net impact of refugee inflows on the German economy will be positive in any case, with benefits outweighing costs for the economy already after five to ten years. The study concludes that the question is when, not whether, refugees will prove to be a long-term gain for the German economy. The blessing, they claim, is assured in any case.[2] The European Commission also takes a carefully optimistic view, with their European Economic Forecast stating that refugees' impact on Germany's economy by 2020 will likely be small, in the order of 0.2-0.3 percent of GDP, but positive even if most of them turn out to be low-skilled.

Such affirmative views are supported by survey findings of the UN Refugee Agency UNHCR that nearly nine out of ten Syrians arriving in Greece report high levels of education, with 43 percent holding a university degree, and another 43 percent a high school diploma.[3] Nearly eight out of ten surveyed Syrians (78 percent) were under 35, and half of them said they wanted to go to Germany, citing employment and educational opportunities among their reasons.[4]

What is the counter-narrative to the optimistic camp? Proponents of the "burden" camp cite competing studies that warn nearly two-thirds of Syrians cannot read or write fluently and have trouble with basic math, as PISA and other international comparative educational studies find.[5] A survey conducted among Syrians in Turkish refugee camps draws similar conclusions, finding that 80 percent of Syrians bring less than a high school education.[6] Germany's Office for Migration and Refugee (BAMF) finds that around half of surveyed Syrians in Germany reported having either university degree or a high-school diploma—but that asylum seekers from other countries brought on average lower levels of education.[7]

Other studies focus on the high cost of refugees. For instance, the Institute for the Global Economy (IfW) in Kiel projects the annual cost of refugees to Germany's economy in the coming years to range between €25 million and €55 million—a burden difficult to debate away, even if the economy does well.[8]

Why Is It So Hard to Estimate Refugees' Impact on the Labor Market?

Why is this question so controversial? Why do we see so many competing studies with widely diverse findings? The answer lies in what we do not know. The economic impact of refugees depends on how well they integrate into the German labor market—and that depends on a lot of factors we do not yet know enough about to make solid predictions. For instance, Germany does not know how many arrivals it will see in the future, nor which countries they will come from. We have estimates, of course, but as flows and origin countries change and as Germany's and its neighbors' policies start to take effect, estimates change. Even if we know which countries people come from, and even if know how old they are and whether they went to school or university, we do not know how those schools' curricula compare to Germany's, and how able and willing each person will be to learn German and apply him or herself in the labor market.

The predictions in studies we currently read are based on widely varying assumptions or, less euphemistically, guesswork. Predicting accurately the impact of the migrant and refugee flows on Germany's labor market in the future is like trying to accurately predict precipitation: Experts come up with generally good estimates, based on factors they can measure and experience they have with weather patterns, but in the end, sometimes there is a 50 percent chance of rain: It may rain, experts say—but it also may not. This does not discard or discredit the studies we have so far, but simply acknowledges their inherent limitations. Experts' predictions are only as good as the data sources they are based on.

Five Factors That Influence Labor Market Integration

The silver lining is not far, though. While there is a lot we do not know, we do know that refugees' integration into the labor market depends on at least five factors.

1. Language

Successful integration hinges on language learning. Gaining and keeping a job, let alone climbing a career ladder, depends on refugees' ability to communicate in German. In many jobs, that does not just include basic language skills to get by, but also profession-specific language, such as medical or technical terms doctors, nurses, or metal workers need.[9] Germany's government promotes language classes as the main element of its federally funded integration courses, providing at least 600 hours of language instruction to new arrivals,[10] and new projects combine profession-specific language training with internships to allow refugees to learn specialized terminology while already gaining work experience.[11] While the existence of such courses shows Germany's political and financial dedication to tackling the language challenge, critics lament an insufficient supply of these courses.

2. Education and Skill Levels

Germany's labor market needs skilled workers, some university-educated, some with a vocational or technical education. Refugees that bring these skills, especially in growth occupations with likely high demand in the future (such as health care and geriatric care workers), have better chances of finding employment and integrating successfully. Those without sufficient education levels need to catch up, by going back to school, updating their skills, or participating in so-called bridge programs that aim to fill the gaps between the skills a person has and those needed to enter employment. Social and cultural skills also matter. Recognizing authority of female bosses, punctuality, and reliability are soft skills German employers expect their workers to have. Unlike thematic knowledge and technical skills, cultural skills need to not just be understood, but internalized.[12]

3. Qualifications Recognition

Even if refugees bring qualifications well matched to the needs of employers, they often need to take the additional step of having them recognized before they are allowed to work. Rigorous recognition processes are a mechanism to protect the public, especially for licensed professions like healthcare workers. Patients seeing a Syrian dentist breathe more freely knowing that she has passed comparable training and exams as a German dentist would have. Germany's foundational law to address this challenge is the so-called Recognition Act of 2012, which mandates that migrants who apply for recognition of their degrees and education in Germany have to receive a decision within three months. A webpage guides applicants through the process and draws a path through the complex jungle of regulating bodies and certificates needed to access different professions. In spite of this progress and success stories of the last years, getting qualifications recognized remains a long and often arduous process.[13] Long wait times lead to de-skilling and lengthen the time refugees depend on government support.

4. Legal Right to Work

Withholding a work permit from refugees is one of the most effective ways to slow down their integration. During the last big refugee wave in the early 1990s, Germany deterred labor market participation of asylum seekers, arguing it would incentivize more people to come. Today's policies do the opposite: they encourage asylum seekers to participate in Germany's labor market, citing the need for early integration, refugees' desire for self-sufficiency, and the high cost of prolonged government support. Asylum seekers receive labor market access after three months, a marked decrease from the nine months they had to wait prior to the so-called asylum compromise of 2014. Their access is non-preferential until 15 months, though, meaning they can only be hired if the Federal Employment Agency gives its okay, which it generally only does if no Germans or EU citizens are available for the job. Full access is gained at the end of 15 months, once more a marked decrease from the four years asylum seekers waited beforehand.[14] These changes are an improvement for asylum seekers' ability to enter the labor market early, but critical voices, including the new head of the Federal Office for Migration and Refugees, argue the one year period of non-preferential treatment should be decreased or temporarily abolished to avoid unnecessary delays.[15]

5. Employer Openness

Without German businesses willing to employ asylum seekers and refugees, labor market integration remains a pipedream. The good news is that German employers have shown increasing openness to hire refugees, and have launched numerous initiatives to integrate them into their workforce. Multinational car manufacturers like Porsche and Daimler offer vocational training programs for refugees, and Germany's Mittelstand, the countless SMEs revered as engine of the country's export power, has also jumped on the bandwagon.[16] Early experiences with these programs have shown that refugees need not just a job, but special support systems. The Munich Chamber of Skilled Crafts, for instance, established a mentoring system to support refugees with challenges of daily life, such as finding an affordable apartment in notoriously expensive Munich, which helped reduce dropout rates from vocational trainings.[17] Since most of these initiatives of German enterprises are only a few months old, it remains to be seen how many refugees will be able to benefit from them and how well they manage to prepare refugees for the demands of German work life.

How to Make Things Better: Recommendations for Germans and Refugees in Germany

So what should we do with this knowledge? How do we influence these five factors positively so they help not hinder refugees' integration?

Overall, German policymakers have launched a host of policies and programs to address these five challenges in recent months and years. But since most of these initiatives are still in their pilot phases, we do not yet know how well they work, nor do they reach enough people. Due to this fact, the recommendations put forward here focus on continuing the first promising steps Germany has made, evaluating them carefully, and scaling them up when possible. Concretely, here is what the German government, businesses, and civil society can do to improve integration of refugees, and what refugees themselves can do.

First, the federal government should continue to expand its language course offerings, both the basic language classes and those teaching profession-specific vocabulary. In the first nine months of 2015, nearly 1,400 language course providers conducted more than 8,000 courses, up 15 percent from the same period in the year prior.[18] Given the parallel increases of arrivals, this development should continue. At the same time, the countless civil society initiatives that bring together volunteers to teach German in the classroom or through language tandems are indispensable in cementing the language skills newcomers learn in the classroom.

Second, carefully evaluate and, if found successful, expand pilot projects that screen asylum seekers' skills already while their claims are processed. Existing evidence, for instance from the "Early Intervention" pilot project the Labor Ministry and Federal Labor Agency (BA) conducts in collaboration with the BAMF, shows that assessing asylum seekers' skills and abilities at an early stage not only allows them to find employment or training more quickly, but also boosts asylum seekers' self-esteem and integration motivation.[19]

Third, continue to provide and expand support to undergo the complex process of qualification recognition. A government webpage helps applicants find the right agency in charge of recognizing their foreign degrees and experience, and another pilot project called "Prototyping Transfer," this time by the Federal Institute for Vocational Education and Training (BIBB), allows refugees without written proof of their qualifications to take tests or provide work samples to prove their skills and knowledge instead. These are steps in the right direction, but they need to continue much further to impact more than a few hundred pilot participants.

Fourth, German policymakers and media should discuss the pros and cons of decreasing or abolishing the non-preferential access period. Critics say it effectively keeps many refugees out of the labor market for 15 months, an unnecessarily long time. Supporters are concerned about social tensions if newcomers stiffen labor market competition and are perceived to decrease wages. Reforms to labor market access need to guard against compounding an "us versus them" mentality that can be fueled by granting benefits too quickly and independently of the validity and outcome of asylum claims.

Fifth, the numerous integration initiatives started by German employers are good steps in the right direction, but would benefit from coordination and evaluation. The recently founded network "Enterprises integrate refugees," supported by the Ministry for the Economy, brings together more than 300 German businesses to exchange good practices and provide practical advice on how to integrate refugees in employment and vocational training.[20] Since many firms' initiatives are recent, they would benefit from advice on how to overcome common hurdles.

Last, the best integration intentions get stretched to breaking point if the number of entries increases unabated, and the German people gets the impression that the many integration resources spent are nothing more than a drop in the bucket. Policymakers across the political spectrum acknowledge that limiting the number of additional entries is desirable to facilitate the successful integration of asylum seekers and refugees already in Germany.

What about the refugees themselves? Having arrived from a long journey to Europe, they have to find the motivation and willingness to dive into a new life in a culture different from their own, including a different work culture. Skilled workers need to accept that they often start at a lower level. Doctors should not work as taxi drivers, but some may end up having to work as nurses or care workers, at least in the beginning. And many refugees will have very low or no relevant skills, or reject basic principles of German society, including gender equality and freedom of religion. Their integration will take much longer, if it succeeds at all. Both sides, Germans and refugees, need to manage their expectations. Integrating the hundreds of thousands of arrivals who will receive protection and stay in Germany will take a long time, and frustrations on both sides are guaranteed.

Growth, personal and societal, always comes with pain. The migration and refugee crisis has triggered a growth spurt of German society, as it has unleashed a wave of controversial discussions about the country's identity. While the rising popularity of the AfD and anti-immigrant movements is often interpreted as a regression of Germany's debate to worse times, it can also be seen as a sign that Germany's migration debate is maturing and becoming more complex. Germany's discussions, which focused mostly on integration concerns during the last decade, are now pushed toward a more diverse conversation, and that includes extreme views any democracy has to be able to withstand.

Integration, the platitude goes, is a two-way street. Both host society and migrants need to adapt their ways for successful integration. Whether refugees turn out to be a burden or a blessing to the German labor market is not a given, it is not yet decided. It is a process in the making—a process both Germans and newcomers can and should shape.

Resources

[1] "Aktuelle Zahlen zu Asyl," Federal Office for Migration and Refugees, February 2016, https://www.bamf.de/SharedDocs/Anlagen/DE/Downloads/Infothek/Statistik/Asyl/statistik-anlage-teil-4-aktuelle-zahlen-zu-asyl.pdf?__blob=publicationFile and http://doku.iab.de/aktuell/2015/aktueller_bericht_1514.pdf

[2] Marcel Fratzscher and Simon Junker, "Integration von Fluechtlingen – eine langfristig lohnende Investition," DIW Wochenbericht, Nr. 45 (2015), http://www.diw.de/sixcms/detail.php?id=diw_01.c.518260.de

[3] http://www.unhcr.org/5666ddda6.html and "Syrian Refugee Arrivals in Greece: Preliminary Questionaire Findings," UNHCR, April-September 2015, data.unhcr.org/mediterranean/download.php?id=248#_ga=1.161302462.222600204.1457214474, p.6.

[4] UNHCR, p.4 and 5

[5] Jan-Martin Wiarda, "Zwei Drittel können kaum lesen und schreiben," Die Zeit, 3 December 2015, http://www.zeit.de/2015/47/integration-fluechtlinge-schule-bildung-herausforderung

[6] Virginia Kirst, "Hälfte der syrischen Flüchtlinge schlecht ausgebildet," Die Welt, 27 October 2015, http://www.welt.de/wirtschaft/article148098162/Haelfte-der-syrischen-Fluechtlinge-schlecht-ausgebildet.html

[7] "Syrer offenbar gebildeter als andere Flüchtlinge," MiGazin, 17 September 2015, http://www.migazin.de/2015/09/17/syrer-offenbar-gebildeter-als-andere-fluechtlinge/ and Jan Dams, "Jeder sechste Flüchtling ging auf die Uni," Die Welt, 28 August 2015, http://www.welt.de/wirtschaft/article145745112/Jeder-sechste-Fluechtling-ging-auf-die-Uni.html

[8] Martin Greive, "Flüchtlingskrise kostet bis zu 55 Milliarden Euro im Jahr," Die Welt, 11 December 2015, http://www.welt.de/wirtschaft/article149854636/Fluechtlingskrise-kostet-bis-zu-55-Milliarden-Euro-im-Jahr.html. The original study is available at: https://www.ifw-kiel.de/

[9] "Wie klappt's in der Praxis?" tagesschau.de, 21 January 2016, http://www.tagesschau.de/inland/integration-107.html

[10] "Integration courses – what are they?" Federal Office for Migration and Refugees, http://www.bamf.de/EN/Willkommen/DeutschLernen/Integrationskurse/integrationskurse-node.html

[11] Britta Beeger, "Mohammeds weiter Weg zu Festanstellung," FAZ.net, 5 October 2015, http://www.faz.net/aktuell/beruf-chance/arbeitswelt/projekt-in-muenchen-zeigt-wie-muehsam-es-ist-fluechtlinge-in-arbeit-zu-bringen-13838228.html and Pressemitteilungen, Horst Seehofer, 13 October 2015, http://www.bayern.de/unterzeichnung-der-vereinbarung-integration-durch-ausbildung-und-arbeit-ministerpraesident-horst-seehofer-zentraler-bestandteil-des-bayerischen-sonderprogramms-zusa/

[12] "Wie klappt's in der Praxis?" tagesschau.de, 21 January 2016, http://www.tagesschau.de/inland/integration-107.html and Monika Bethscheider, "Interkulturelle Kompetenz – der Schlüssel für gelingende Integration im Betrieb?" BiBB Qualiboxx,

9 February 2016, https://www.qualiboxx.de/wws/interkulturelle-kompetenz.php?s id=15108796801041194445876267626510

[13] "Recognition in Germany," Federal Ministry of Education and Research, https://www.anerkennung-in-deutschland.de/html/en/success_stories.php

[14] "Erleichterungen für Asylbewerber," Website of the Federal Government, https://www.bundesregierung.de/Content/DE/Artikel/2014/10/2014-10-29-verbesserungen-fuer-asylbewerber-beschlossen.html and "Arbeitsmarktzugangsmöglichkeiten für Flüchtlinge," Federal Ministry of Labor and Social Affairs, http://www.bmas.de/DE/Schwerpunkte/Neustart-in-Deutschland/Neustart-Asylsuchende/arbeitsmarktzugang-asylbewerber-geduldete.html and Roland Preuß, "So sieht der Asylkompromiss aus," Süddeutsche Zeitung, 22 September 2014, http://www.sueddeutsche.de/politik/herkunftsstaaten-und-residenzpflicht-so-sieht-der-asylkompromiss-aus-1.2137533 and "Welchen Effekt haben Flüchtlinge auf den Arbeitsmarkt?" Medien Dienst Integration, 29 October 2015, https://mediendienst-integration.de/artikel/fluechtlinge-arbeitsmarkt-berufliche-integration-early-intervention.html

[15] "Pause bei Vorrangprüfung: Arbeitsagentur will Flüchtlingen Zugang zu Jobs erleichtern," Spiegel Online, 1 September 2015, http://www.spiegel.de/wirtschaft/soziales/asylbewerber-bundesagentur-will-vorrangpruefung-aussetzen-a-1050898.html and "De Maziere und Weise uneins bei Vorrangsprüfung," Die Welt, 21 September 2015, http://www.welt.de/politik/deutschland/article146639309/De-Maiziere-und-Weise-uneins-bei-Vorrangpruefung.html

[16] "Beispielhafte Integrationsprojekte," Wirtschaft Zusammen: Integrations-Initiativen der Deutschen Wirtschaft, http://wir-zusammen.de/patenschaften and Hanna Spanhel and Lea Lehner, "Integration an der Werkbank," Stuttgarter Nachrichten, 9 March 2016, http://www.stuttgarter-nachrichten.de/inhalt.fluechtlinge-bei-porsche-integration-an-der-werkbank.d5d84cc9-5eb3-44af-8e21-f780701e07b3.html

[17] "Wie klappt's in der Praxis?" tagesschau.de, 21 January 2016, http://www.tagesschau.de/inland/integration-107.html

[18] "Geschäftsstatistik zum Integrationskurs," Federal Office for Migration and Refugees, http://www.bamf.de/DE/Infothek/Statistiken/InGe/inge-node.html

[19] Volker Daumann, et. al., "Early Intervention – Modellprojekt zur Frühzeitigen Arbetismarktintegration von Asylbewerberinnen und Asylbewerbern," IAB Forschungsbericht 3/2015, http://doku.iab.de/forschungsbericht/2015/fb0315.pdf

[20] See https://www.unternehmen-integrieren-fluechtlinge.de/netzwerk/

Refugees Need Work Opportunities

International Labour Organization

In the following excerpted viewpoint, the International Labour Organization explores how the Syrian refugee crisis is affecting neighboring countries. Negative impacts include rising unemployment, poor wages and working conditions, and child labor. The report suggests that the international community needs to do more to ensure decent work opportunities to these immigrants. It describes specific challenges and suggestions for improving the labor market and economies in the host countries. The International Labour Organization is a United Nations agency that works with governments, employers, and workers representatives to promote decent work for all women and men.

As you read, consider the following questions:

1. What percentage of people living in Lebanon are refugees?
2. What are the five principal host countries for Syrian refugees?
3. What happens to the economy when host countries receive large numbers of new refugees?

"The ILO Response To The Syrian Refugee Crisis," International Labour Organization, February 2016. Reprinted by Permission ©2016, ILO.

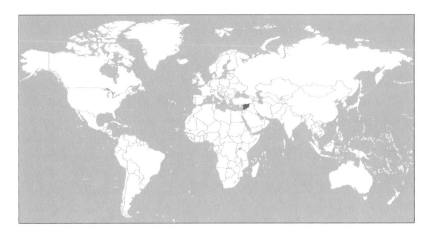

Context

Almost five years into the Syrian conflict, the ensuing refugee crisis remains one of the largest, most protracted and complex humanitarian emergencies of modern times. According to UNHCR registration data, more than 4.1 million Syrians have now fled their country. Jordan – with its population of 6.4 million – has an expanding Syrian refugee population of more than 620,000 women, men and their families. In Lebanon the refugee influx has taken on dramatic proportions: in October 2015 it was estimated that close to 1.1 million registered Syrian refugees lived in Lebanon.1 To this, hundreds of thousands unregistered refugees may have to be added: refugees now account for one in four people living in Lebanon. In Turkey there are nearly 2.1 million officially registered Syrian refugees; in Egypt 130,000; and in Iraq almost 250,000.[2]

The effects of the Syrian refugee crisis are increasingly spilling over into the economic and social spheres – leading to stalled economic activity, loss of income, and shrinking access to quality public services in host countries that already had to contend with difficult socioeconomic conditions before the crisis began. Today, and in many ways, the crisis can be seen as a test for the accomplishment of the ambitious and transformative 2030 Agenda for Sustainable Development – and its accompanying goals.

Against this backdrop, the Regional Refugee Response and Resilience Plan (3RP) in response to the Syria crisis was launched by the United Nations in December 2014. The 3RP is a country-driven, regionally coherent plan to address refugee protection and humanitarian needs, build the resilience of vulnerable people and impacted host communities and strengthen the capacity of national delivery systems in the five most affected countries neighbouring Syria. The 3RP is central to the impact and sustainability of the response going forward and its success demands much more effective and efficient collaboration between UN agencies and international organizations. This Plan integrates and is aligned with existing and emerging national plans, including the Jordan Response Plan (JRP) 2015, the Lebanon Crisis Response Plan (LCRP), the Iraq Strategic Response Plan (SRP), and country responses in Turkey and Egypt.

[…]

Impact of the Crisis on the Labour Market

The Syrian conflict has had a discernible impact on the labour markets of recipient refugee countries, such as Jordan and Lebanon – countries that were already experiencing difficult economic conditions before the refugee crisis began. Recipient countries face dramatic increases in the labour supply –putting considerable pressure on their fragile labour markets and aggravating pre-existing economic difficulties. While the socio-economic and labour market situations of the affected countries differ in many ways, the refugee crisis has had the following consequences:

- Rising unemployment, with a considerable impact on young people and unskilled workers

- Competition, pressure on wages and deteriorating working conditions, with an increase in informal employment

- Worst forms of child labour among refugees are on the rise, with evidence of forced labour emerging

- The depletion of livelihoods in host community economies

Illegal Immigration and Public Health

There's a growing health concern over illegal immigrants bringing infectious diseases into the United States. Approximately 500,000 legal immigrants and 80,000 refugees come to the United States each year, and an additional 700,000 illegal immigrants enter annually, and three-quarters of these illegal immigrants come from Mexico, El Salvador, Guatemala, and Honduras.

Legal immigrants and refugees are required to have a medical examination for migration to the United States, while they are still overseas. … Individuals who fail the exam due to certain health-related conditions are not admitted to the United States. … Illegal immigrants crossing into the United States could bring any of these threats, however. Southern Texas Border Patrol agent Chris Cabrera warns: "What's coming over into the US could harm everyone. We are starting to see scabies, chicken pox, methicillin-resistant Staphylococcus aureus infections, and different viruses."

Illegal immigration may expose Americans to diseases that have been virtually eradicated, but are highly contagious, as in the case of TB. This disease rose by 20% globally from 1985 to 1991, and was declared a worldwide emergency by the World Health Organization (WHO) in 1995. Furthermore, TB frequently occurs in connection with the human immunodeficiency virus. Fortunately, more than 90% of Central Americans are vaccinated against TB, according to the WHO.

The federal government's Department of Homeland Security has public health controls in place to minimize any possible health risks, including medical units at the busiest border stations and measures to protect Customs and Border Protection including gloves, long-sleeve shirts, and frequent hand washing. In addition, the CDC's Division of Global Migration and Quarantine has measures in place to protect the population from communicable diseases. The agency works through a variety of activities to prevent the introduction, transmission, and spread of communicable diseases in the United States.

"Illegal Immigration and the Threat of Infectious Disease," Content Editor, Southern Medical Association, February 18, 2015.

- Weak labour market governance and capacity of governments to adequately respond to the situation

The ILO Strategy

A large portion of the international community's response to the ongoing Syrian crisis has overwhelmingly focused on humanitarian aspects, and the livelihoods component of the Regional Refugee and Resilience Plan 2015 - 2016 (3RP) has so far received the least attention. Should a greater inward investment in decent work and livelihoods not be mobilized, the negative consequences of the crisis will continue and deepen. Livelihoods must be linked to local economic development plans, while engaging the private sector in a more meaningful manner.

More recently, however, and due to the protracted nature of the crisis, the focus has indeed been shifting towards a more integrated approach that brings together both the humanitarian and development aspects of the crisis under one framework. The resilience agenda emanating from this approach and clearly articulated in the 3RP represents efforts by a wide range of national and international partners towards a more effective and sustainable response which strengthens the resilience and stability of countries and communities affected by the crisis.

To this end, the ILO strategy[4] is development-focused and employment-driven in its support to host communities and refugees so as to maintain and reinforce the social and economic stability of the affected neighbouring countries.

The multi-faceted nature of the crisis cuts across many of the ILO's interventions and new initiatives that complement existing country programmes, which are already focused on expanding decent work opportunities, addressing child labour, extending social protection and enhancing employment for young women and men.

The ILO strategy builds on its core mandate to promote employment, social dialogue, social protection and rights at work. It consists of three key pillars:

1. Supporting evidence-based policy development to ensure an employment-rich national response, embedded in the principles of decent work;

2. Contributing to building the resilience of host communities by enhancing access to employment opportunities and livelihoods;

3. Strengthening institutional capacities and coordination to combat unacceptable forms of work, with a focus on child labour.

In implementing this strategy, the ILO works closely with other UN agencies and Bretton Woods institutions, including the Office of the United Nations High Commissioner for Refugees (UNHCR), the United Nations Development Programme (UNDP), the Food and Agriculture Organization of the United Nations (FAO), the United Nations Children Fund (UNICEF), the United Nations Industrial Development Organization (UNIDO), and the World Bank.

Within this context, the ILO organized a high-level regional dialogue (Istanbul, Turkey, 28-29 July 2015) which brought together representatives from the five principal host countries (Jordan, Lebanon, Turkey, Egypt and Iraq) and a range of international partners – with a view to assessing the effects of the refugee influx on national and local labour markets and exchanging experiences on appropriate responses and the mechanisms being applied by different host countries to Syrian refugees' access to work. This meeting served as a key means of strengthening coordination between tripartite constituents (workers, employers and governments) for better analysis and better responses to the crisis – at national and regional levels.

By virtue of this dialogue, a range of forward-looking recommendations aimed at informing policy formulation, programme development, and continual dialogue were articulated, cementing the ILO's role in this response. These recommendations also suggested the roles that affected governments, social partners and the international community could play to contribute to the livelihoods component of the Regional Plan (3RP) and offer decent work opportunities to all women and men in the affected countries.[5] The ILO strategy is centred on the following approaches:

- Investing in the capacity and ownership of local actors in the identification of and support to local economic development, including value chain development and income generation projects in crisis affected areas, which can benefit both host communities and the refugees.

- Implementing projects in selected sectors and governorates by enhancing employment services, and supporting business development and livelihoods projects, which leads to tangible short-term employment opportunities with longer-term prospects. These projects will have the potential to be scaled up and handed over to national and local entities for longer-term gains. A practical example is the Employment Intensive Investment Programmes (EIIP) approach, which includes implementing specific labour-intensive works to increase public asset value and improve the general economic situation.

- Helping improve the regulation of the presence of Syrian workers in the labour market by introducing job placement mechanisms and promoting measures preventing unacceptable working conditions (in terms of wages, occupational safety and health, etc.), including through negotiated social monitoring among host and refugee communities and enhanced labour inspection capacity. The ILO will also explore the application of the ILO's Transition from the Informal to the Formal Economy Recommendation, 2015 (No. 204) to the context of the Syrian crisis, as well as the wider application of the ILO's normative framework, particularly core labour standards.

- Promoting better linkages between national and humanitarian responses to Syrian child labour by ensuring stronger coherence and more effective coordination with the National

Frameworks and Plans to combat child labour, especially in its worst forms.

- Providing policy development support to governments and national or international partners on active labour market programmes, as well as entrepreneurship development and the identification of employment opportunities available in national labour markets, including those created by the "aid economy". To this end, the ILO leverages experience and expertise in vocational education and accreditation frameworks that can support the labour mobility of refugee and national workers. Through this initiative, the ILO also ensures linkages and complementarity with existing development plans, such as the National Employment Strategy in Jordan.

- Fostering social dialogue focusing on refugees' access to employment and labour markets and collective representation. To this end, the ILO has been in regular dialogue with national policy makers, social partners, and development partners on how to provide access to work for Syrian refugees and creating a win-win situation that yields social and economic dividends for the host economies. For instance, together with UNHCR and UNDP, it is now engaged in preparing a white paper on access to labour markets in Jordan.

- Stimulating regional cooperation between the most affected countries and the international community, including the UN system. To this end, the ILO convened the regional dialogue on the labour market impact of the Syrian refugee crisis in Jordan, Lebanon, Turkey, Iraq and Egypt (Istanbul, July 2015 – see above).

- Promoting "resilience inside Syria", in line with the international community's new approach. The ILO is exploring ways to reactivate its development cooperation programme in Syria as a means of providing livelihoods and social protection to vulnerable members of the population, in particular displaced persons. Recently, the ILO has been engaged in a dialogue with constituents on possible entry points for reengagement, particularly in the areas of employment policy and labour market information, emergency employment and livelihood recovery, workers' protection, and social security, as well as child and forced labour.

[…]

Programme Outline: Jordan

By January 2016 the number of registered Syrian refugees in Jordan had exceeded 635,000. 6 While around 20 per cent of refugees currently live in designated camps in Jordan, the rest have found shelter in cities and rural areas across the Kingdom. Amman and the northern governorates of Irbid and Mafraq alone host more than 73 per cent of the total number of Syrian refugees in the country.[7] As the conflict approaches its fifth year, a number of studies have revealed the crisis' significant impact on the Jordanian labour market. There are strong concerns about the effects on wage levels, working conditions, child labour and informal work, and rising social tension over job competition.

According to a 2015 ILO survey only 51 per cent of Syrian men (and 7 per cent of women) who live outside refugee camps participate in the Jordanian labour market with an unemployment rate as high as 57 per cent. 90 per cent of Syrian refugees working outside camps do not have work permits and are as such employed in the informal economy and outside the bounds of Jordanian labour law. This reinforces the current trend towards the expansion of Jordanian informal employment, which is characterised by low and declining wages, long working days, and poor working conditions and regulations, including lack of proper work contracts.[8] Child labour also disproportionately affects Syrian children living outside camps. Only 1.6 per cent of Jordanian boys in the age group 9-15 are economically active, compared to more than 8 per cent of Syrian boys in the same age group. These figures rise to 37 per cent of Syrian boys, compared to 17 per cent of Jordanian boys, for the age group 15-18.

[…]

Programme Outline: Turkey

Turkey has, since the beginning of the Syrian crisis in 2011, provided an effective emergency response and declared a temporary protection regime for Syrian refugees, ensuring both protection and assistance in 23 camps set up by the Disaster and Emergency Management Agency (AFAD). As of 2 October 2015, Turkey hosts almost 2.1 million registered Syrian refugees. Around 250,000 refugees reside in camps, while over 1.5 million live within host communities. Most camp refugees live in the south (Adana, Hatay, Osmaniye, and Kahramanmaraş) and south-east (Adıyaman, Gaziantep, Kilis, Mardin, Şanlıurfa) of Turkey. Other major cities such as Istanbul, Konya and Mersin have seen an increase in the number of Syrians. 74 of 81 provinces in Turkey currently host Syrian refugees.

As the conflict approaches its fifth year, the influx can be seen to have had a significant impact on the Turkish labour market. There is no systematic assessment of the impact of the crisis on the socioeconomic situation at national and local levels, but only limited sample-based information exists on the income levels of the Syrian refugees in and outside camps, based on a study carried out by AFAD.[20] According to this report, over half of the refugees who live and work in Turkish communities earn less than USD 250 a month, far less than the minimum wage in Turkey. Limited information is available on the working conditions of Syrian workers currently making their living through informal jobs. The pressure on the local economy and on the Government to provide jobs and services has grown, causing discontent among the host communities. Competition between Syrians and Turkish nationals has increased, especially for low-skilled jobs, and this creates downward pressure on wages. Syrian workers tend to work in poor working conditions where core labour and social rights are not observed, in seasonal agricultural and low-skilled jobs. Local level consultations show that wages and fees have dropped to one-fifth of their previous levels, causing the working conditions of the most vulnerable groups from both communities to deteriorate, including children not in school.

The Government of Turkey has taken swift action to accommodate Syrian refugees. The "Law on Foreigners and International Protection" was adopted in April 2013, followed by the adoption of a "Temporary Protection Regulation" (TP) in 2014, which provides the legal and administrative framework for the protection and assistance of persons in need of international protection. The regulation provides Syrian refugees with rights and duties, and a framework for access to health care, education, the labour market and social assistance. The TP enables refugees' access to the labour market, as it allows for registered and documented Syrian refugees to apply for work permits in defined sectors, professions and geographical areas. For this purpose a second set of regulations to govern working conditions for Syrian refugees has been prepared by the Ministry of Labour and Social Security (MoLSS) and submitted to the Council of Ministers for approval.

Endnotes

1 Since 6 May 2015, UNHCR Lebanon has temporarily suspended new registration in accordance with the Government's instructions. Women, men, girls and boys awaiting registration are hence no longer included.

2 For up to date UNHCR figures on Syria Regional Refugee Response, please see: http://data.unhcr.org/syrianrefugees/regional.php

3 Please see: http://www.ilo.org/beirut/country/lang--en/index.htm.

4 For more information, including multimedia products on the ILO's response to the Syria crisis, please see: http://www.ilo.org/beirut/areasofwork/syrian-refugee-crisis/lang--en/index.htm

5 For more information about the high-level regional dialogue, please see: http://www.ilo.org/beirut/publications/WCMS_408999/lang--en/index.htm

6 ILO (2014) The Impact of the Syrian Refugee Crisis on the Labour market in Jordan: a Preliminary Analysis (http://www.ilo.org/wcmsp5/groups/public/---arabstates/---ro-beirut/documents/publication/wcms_242021.pdf) For more information, see also: http://data.unhcr.org/syrianrefugees/country.php?id=107.

7 These estimates are based on UNHCR statistics of Syrian refugees in Jordan (http://data.unhcr.org/syrianrefugees/country.php?id=107) and DoS Population Statistics for 2011, (http://www.dos.gov.jo/dos_home_e/main/).

8 ILO/Fafo/DOS (2015) Impact of the influx of Syrian refugees on the Jordanian labour market: findings from the governorates of Amman, Irbid and Magraq. (See: http://www.ilo.org/beirut/publications/WCMS_364162/lang-- en/index.htm)

10 Please see: http://www.data.unhcr.org/syrianrefugees/country.php?id=122.

11 ILO. 2015, Towards Decent Work in Lebanon: Issues and Challenges in Light of the Syrian Refugee Crisis

12 World Bank. 2015, Lebanon: Promoting Poverty Reduction and Shared Prosperity. A Systemic Country Diagnostic.

13 ILO. 2015, Towards Decent Work in Lebanon: Issues and Challenges in Light of the Syrian Refugee Crisis.

14 The World Bank (See: the World Bank. 2013. Economic and Social Impact Assessment of the Syrian Conflict) estimated that the unemployment rate would reach 20 per cent by the end of 2014. A revision of this assessment is necessary due to the fact that the demographic shock of the crisis was not as high as expected.

15 World Bank. 2015, Lebanon: Promoting Poverty Reduction and Shared Prosperity. A Systemic Country Diagnostic.

16 VaSyr 2015. Preliminary results.

17 ILO. 2014. Assessment of the Impact of Syrian Refugees in Lebanon and their Employment Profile.

18 ILO. 2014. Assessment of the impact of Syrian refugees in Lebanon and their Employment Profile, and OCHA-REACHUNICEF. 2015. Defining Community Vulnerability in Lebanon.

19 The LCRP is Lebanon's country plan part of the Regional Refugee and Resilience Plan 2015-16. For more information, please see: http://www.unocha.org/cap/appeals/lebanon-crisis-response-plan-2015-2016.

Immigrants Bring Economic Benefits but Security Risks

Tim Kane and Kirk A. Johnson

In the following viewpoint, Tim Kane and Kirk A. Johnson claim that US immigration policies require greater reform. They believe that immigration is generally positive, but reform should include both border security and the economy. They see the primary problem with illegal immigration as security, because terrorists and drug traffickers find it easier to hide. They believe the answer is an improved guest worker program. Tim Kane and Kirk A. Johnson were writing on behalf of The Heritage Foundation, a conservative research center.

As you read, consider the following questions:

1. What percentage of people in America was undocumented immigrants at the time of this writing?
2. What percentage of the US population was foreign-born Americans?
3. How did the immigrant unemployment rate compare to the national average?

America's exceptional status as a "nation of immigrants" is being challenged by globalization, which is making both migration and terrorism much easier. The biggest challenge for policymakers is distinguishing illusory immigration problems from real problems.

"The Real Problem with Immigration... and the Real Solution," by Tim Kane and Kirk A. Johnson, The Heritage Foundation, March 1, 2006. Reprinted by permission.

One thing is quite clear: The favored approach of recent years-a policy of benign neglect-is no longer tenable. Members of both the Senate and the House of Representatives recognize this and deserve credit for striving to craft a comprehensive law during this session of Congress.

In 2005, immigration policy received far more genuine attention on Capitol Hill, and Members of Congress from both sides of the aisle are now considering what to do about immigration policy. Their various efforts have focused on a wide variety of changes in current policy, including improving border security, strengthening employer verification of employment, establishing a new temporary guest worker program, and offering some level of amnesty to illegal immigrants currently living in the United States. At present, these proposals are working their way through the legislative process.

However, to achieve results, immigration reform must be comprehensive. A lopsided, ideological approach that focuses exclusively on border security while ignoring migrant workers (or vice versa) is bound to fail. If Congress passes another law that glosses over the fundamental contradictions in the status quo, then the status quo will not change. Thinking through the incentives is the key to success.

The Real Problem

Illegal immigration into the United States is massive in scale. More than 10 million undocumented aliens currently reside in the U.S., and that population is growing by 700,000 per year.[1] On one hand, the presence of so many aliens is a powerful testament to the attractiveness of America. On the other hand, it is a sign of how dangerously open our borders are.

Typical illegal aliens come to America primarily for better jobs and in the process add value to the U.S. economy. However, they also take away value by weakening the legal and national security environment. When three out of every 100 people in America are undocumented (or, rather, documented with forged and faked papers), there is a profound security problem. Even though they pose no direct security threat, the presence of millions of undocumented migrants distorts the law, distracts resources, and effectively creates a cover for terrorists and criminals.

In other words, the real problem presented by illegal immigration is security, not the supposed threat to the economy. Indeed, efforts to curtail the economic influx of migrants actually worsen the security dilemma by driving many migrant workers underground, thereby encouraging the culture of illegality. A non-citizen guest worker program is an essential component of securing the border, but only if it is the right program.

It is important to craft a guest worker program intelligently. While there are numerous issues involved in such a program, many of which are beyond the scope of this paper, the evidence indicates that worker migration is a net plus economically. With this in mind, there are 14 principles- with an eye toward the economic incentives involved-that should be included as part of a guest worker program.

Immigration Benefits and Costs

An honest assessment acknowledges that illegal immigrants bring real benefits to the supply side of the American economy, which is why the business community is opposed to a simple crackdown.

There are economic costs as well, given America's generous social insurance institutions. The cost of securing the border would logically exist regardless of the number of immigrants.

The argument that immigrants harm the American economy should be dismissed out of hand. The population today includes a far higher percentage (12 percent) of foreign-born Americans than in recent decades, yet the economy is strong, with higher total gross domestic product (GDP), higher GDP per person, higher productivity per worker, and more Americans working than ever before. Immigration may not have caused this economic boom, but it is folly to blame immigrants for hurting the economy at a time when the economy is simply not hurting. As Stephen Moore pointed out in a recent article in *The Wall Street Journal*:

> The increase in the immigration flow has corresponded with steady and substantial reductions in unemployment from 7.3 percent to 5.1 percent over the past two decades. And the unemployment rates have fallen by 6 percentage points for blacks and 3.5 percentage points for Latinos.[2]

Whether low-skilled or high-skilled, immigrants boost national output, enhance specialization, and provide a net economic benefit. The 2005 Economic Report of the President (ERP) devotes an entire chapter to immigration and reports that "A comprehensive accounting of the benefits and costs of immigration shows the benefits of immigration exceed the costs."[3] The following are among the ERP's other related findings:

- Immigrant unemployment rates are lower than the national average in the U.S.;

- Studies show that a 10 percent share increase of immigrant labor results in roughly a 1 percent reduction in native wages-a very minor effect;

- Most immigrant families have a positive net fiscal impact on the U.S., adding $88,000 more in tax revenues than they consume in services; and

- Social Security payroll taxes paid by improperly identified (undocumented) workers have led to a $463 billion funding surplus.

The macroeconomic argument in favor of immigration is especially compelling for highly educated individuals with backgrounds in science, engineering, and information technology. The increasing worry about outsourcing jobs to other nations is just one more reason to attract more jobs to America by insourcing labor. If workers are allowed to work inside the U.S., they immediately add to the economy and pay taxes, which does not happen when a job is outsourced. Therefore, capping the number of H-1B visas limits America's power as a brain "magnet" attracting highly skilled workers, thereby weakening U.S. firms' competitiveness.

Congress increased the number of H-1B visas by 20,000 in November 2004 after the annual cap was exhausted on the first day of fiscal year (FY) 2005.[4] On August 12, 2005, the U.S. citizenship and immigration Service announced that it had already received enough H-1B applications for FY 2006 (which began October 1, 2005) and would not be accepting any more applications for the general selection lottery.[5] These and other numbers show that more workers from abroad, not fewer, are needed.

Still, critics of this type of insourcing worry that jobs are being taken away from native-born Americans in favor of low-wage foreigners. Recent data suggest that these fears are overblown. While the nation's unemployment rate generally has remained just above 5 percent over the past year, unemployment in information technology now stands at a four-year low of 3.7 percent.[6]

While the presence of low-skill migrant workers can be construed as a challenge to low-skill native workers, the economic effects are the same as the effects of free trade-a net positive and a leading cause of economic growth. A National Bureau of Economic Research study by David Card found that "Overall, evidence that immigrants have harmed the opportunities of less educated natives is scant."[7] The consensus of the vast majority of economists is that the broad economic gains from openness to trade and immigration

One View on Immigration and Unemployment

Why do we have immigration when unemployment is high? Nobody in Washington will give the honest answer. Employers want cheap labor. They benefit tremendously from legal and illegal immigration in the current slow-growth economy. We have a million legal immigrants per year, and the vast majority of them enter the labor market competing with Americans for scarce job opportunities. The result is wage depression, though there are other factors that restrict wage growth, and persistently high unemployment above the 5 percent level that most economists believe is unhealthy.

Rather than have a million legal immigrants plus more than three hundred thousand more job seekers coming over on temporary work visas year in and year out without a pause, we should ask the simple question, do we need any immigrants? The only constituency that claims there is such a need is employers. And they have essentially written U.S. immigration law for a very long time.

The primary type of immigration is for "family reunification." That means a U.S. citizen can sponsor their immediate relatives for permanent residency and then citizenship. This sounds like a perfectly reasonable basis on which to base an immigration policy. But it makes no economic sense and has disastrous consequences. Spouses, children and parents of citizens may be unskilled, uneducated, and thus likely to become "public charges," the bane of immigration. Economists agree that the U.S. has ample unskilled labor.

[...]

"Why More Immigration Is Bad for America," by Howard W. Foster, September 5, 2014.

far outweigh the isolated cases of economic loss. In the long run, as has been documented in recent years, the gains are even higher.[8]

A simple example is instructive in terms of both trade and immigration. An imaginary small town has 10 citizens: some farmers, some ranchers, a fisherman, a tailor, a barber, a cook, and a merchant. A new family headed by a young farmer moves to town. His presence is resented by the other farmers, but he also consumes from the other business in town-getting haircuts, eating beef and fish, having his shirts sewn and pressed, and buying supplies at the store, not to mention paying taxes. He undoubtedly boosts the supply side of the economy, but he also boosts the demand side. If he were run out of town for "stealing jobs," his demand for everyone's work would leave with him.

The real problem with undocumented immigrant workers is that flouting the law has become the norm, which makes the job of terrorists and drug traffickers infinitely easier. The economic costs of terrorism can be very high and very real, quite apart from the otherwise positive economic impact of immigration. In order to separate the good from the bad, there is no substitute for a nationwide system that identifies all foreign persons present within the U.S. It is not sufficient to identify visitors upon entry and exit; rather, all foreign visitors must be quickly documented.

Economic Principles for an Effective Guest Worker Program

To this end, 14 economic principles should be borne in mind in crafting an effective guest worker program:

1. **All guest workers in the U.S. should be identified biometrically.** Technologically, a nationwide system of biometric identification (fingerprints, retina scans, etc.) for visitors has already been developed for the US-VISIT program. A sister "WORKER-VISIT" program is essential for enforcement efforts and would help American companies to authenticate guest workers efficiently. There is at present no effective system of internal enforcement, but the Department of Homeland Security (DHS) has in place a "basic pilot employment verification program"[9] that demonstrates the potential effectiveness of using such technology with guest workers to discourage undocumented work arrangements. Employers who want to hire guest workers should be required to verify

electronically that the particular worker has registered with WORKER-VISIT and is eligible to work in the United States.

2. **Existing migrant workers should have incentives to register with the guest worker program.** A guest worker program that is less attractive to migrant workers than the status quo will fail. Therefore, the new law for guest workers should include both positive incentives for compliance and negative incentives (punishments) for non-compliance. For example, a program that caps the tenure of guest workers at six years can be expected to experience massive noncompliance at the six-year point because a hard cap on tenure is essentially an incentive to skirt the law. If the goal is to limit the number of undocumented foreign workers, then renewable short-term work permits have a greater likelihood of success than a single permit with an inflexible expiration date.

3. **U.S. companies need incentives to make the program work.** Immigration reform will be successful if-and probably only if-American companies support its passage and enforcement. A new law must therefore avoid both onerous red tape (e.g., requiring an exhaustive search of native workers before a job can be offered to migrants) and any provision that would make it easier to hire guest workers than it is to hire natives (e.g., waiving payroll taxes on guest workers that must be paid on native worker payrolls). Perhaps the most important incentive is a negative one: The new law should include funding for a system of internal enforcement to police and prosecute companies that break the law.

4. **Guest worker status should not be a path to citizenship and should not include rights to U.S. social benefits.** If the incentive to work in the U.S. is artificially enhanced with a promise of potential citizenship, foreign migrants will be oversupplied. citizenship carries with it tremendous benefits

(e.g., social spending and entitlement programs) that should be provided only to American citizens. For example, unemployment insurance benefits should never go to foreign visitors. Providing benefits such as unemployment insurance, welfare, Head Start, and other payments to visiting workers will significantly distort the incentives to migrate to the U.S. The legal status equivalent of guest workers is that of tourists-people who reside in America temporarily and are bound by U.S. law but do not have any claim on citizenship or its benefits.

5. **Efficient legal entry for guest workers is a necessary condition for compliance.** Existing illegal migrants should be required to leave the U.S. and then allowed a system of entry through border checkpoints with strict conditions for identification, documentation, and compliance with U.S. law. If the guest worker program instead involves prolonged waits for reentry or a lottery for work visas, existing migrant workers will have little incentive to comply with the law. Moreover, such reforms will be perceived as attempts to shrink the supply of migrant labor and will be resisted. However, a program of efficient legal entry for migrants who comply with biometric identification will not deter compliance and will encourage migrants to utilize the formal channels of entry rather than jumping the border.

6. **Efficient legal entry should be contingent upon a brief waiting period** to allow law enforcement agencies the time needed to screen incoming workers. A waiting period of at least a few days will give law enforcement agencies time to screen incoming visitors' biometrics against criminal and terrorist databases.

7. **Provisions for efficient legal entry will not be amnesty,** nor will they "open the floodgates." Such a system will actually encourage many migrants to exit, knowing that they will be able to return under reasonable regulations. This is in stark contrast to the status quo, in which the

difficulty and uncertainty of reentering the U.S. effectively discourage aliens from leaving. Documented migrant workers would enter a new status: not citizen, not illegal, but rather temporary workers. As for opening the floodgates, the reality is that they are already open. More to the point, labor markets operate effectively to balance supply and demand, and those markets are currently in balance. Creating a new category of legal migrants would not change that equilibrium, provide unfair benefits to undocumented aliens over others, or be tied to citizenship, but it would enhance security.

8. **Government agencies should not micromanage migrant labor.** Any federal attempt to license migrants by occupation-micromanaging the market for migrant labor-would be a dangerous precedent and would likely fail. Socialized planning of any market is inferior to the free market, and its implementation is dangerous on many levels. First, allowing government management of the migrant labor market would be terrible precedent for later intrusion into all U.S. labor markets. Second, it would be open to abuse, vulnerable to corruption, and inefficient even if run by angels. For example, in the case of a worker certified as an avocado picker who has carpentry skills that his employer would like to utilize and promote, why should the worker and his employer have to petition a labor Department bureaucrat just to revise the worker's skill certification? Equally implausible is a program that requires migrants and businesses to know one another prior to entry and file the relevant paperwork. Labor markets do not work this way. Such schemes would quickly prove ineffective and lead right back the status quo. Real labor markets work informally, and the power of the market should be utilized to make the guest worker program function efficiently.

9. **The guest worker program should not be used as an excuse to create another large federal bureaucracy.** The

inherent risk of authorizing a new guest worker program is that it will establish a new, unwieldy federal bureaucracy that outgrows its budget and mandate. Critics contend that the federal government is ill-equipped to handle the substantial influx of people who would enter the U.S. through a guest worker program. They further cite the long backlogs that plague other immigration programs, most notably the green card program. One way to alleviate this problem is to involve the private sector in the guest worker visa process, much as gun retailers are integrated into the criminal background checks of gun buyers. Many parts of the guest worker visa process could be facilitated by contracting out certain parts of the process, including paperwork processing, interviewing of visa candidates (if necessary), coordinating with the DHS and federal law enforcement agencies on background checks, facilitating placement with prospective employers, and facilitating the exit upon expiration of the visa. As long as the private contractor has no conflict of interest in the visa selection or placement process, such a system should be better than another federal bureaucracy.

10. **Bonds should be used to promote compliance after entry.** There are many smart ways that bonds could be used to manage the immigrant pool. In one system, guest workers would pay upon entry for a bond that is redeemable upon exit. An individual who wanted to recoup the money would comply with the overall guest worker system and other U.S. laws, effectively acting as part of a self-enforcing network that discourages non-bonded, undocumented migrants. An alternative arrangement would have U.S. companies paying for the bonds as a right to hire some number of workers. If Congress felt compelled to cap the number of guest workers, the bonds could be treated like property rights and bid on to establish the market value of a guest worker. In both cases, the dollar value of the bond would be repaid

after the migrant exited the U.S. but would be forfeit if the migrant went into the black market economy.

11. **Guest workers should be required to find a sponsoring employer** within one month (or some other reasonable period of time). The employer would verify via WORKER-VISIT that the particular worker is eligible to be employed in the United States. If the migrant cannot locate an employer within the time frame, the law should require that he or she leave the country. A sponsorship system is an efficient alternative to government management of the supply of and demand for migrant labor. It would be self-checking because employers could be required to submit payroll records regularly for automated review, which would identify the guest workers at each location. If employment with a sponsor ended, the worker would be allowed a similar reasonable period of time to find a new employer. Existing undocumented workers should find it relatively easy to get sponsorship with current employers, so the act of leaving the country and reentering would neither discourage their compliance nor come at the expense of legal migrants.

12. **Day laborers should be required to find long-term sponsoring employers.** The presence of tens of thousands of day laborers in the U.S.[10] may seem to pose a challenge to immigration reform, but the day labor market should not be given an exemption. A functioning WORKER-VISIT program would likely motivate the creation of intermediary firms that employ day laborers and connect them with customers in a more formal market that develops along the lines of subcontracting firms that are already active in gardening, house-cleaning, janitorial services, accounting, and night security. Intermediary firms could offer day laborers in teams of variable sizes, allowing the hiring firms to avoid the hassles of sponsoring and documentation paperwork. Skeptics might protest that most subcontracted

jobs are routine (even regularly scheduled), whereas day labor is by nature last-minute and unpredictable. However, that is not really true in the aggregate, especially when compared with other last-minute industries like plumbing/flood control or emergency towing. Competitive firms can meet demand with very little slack as long as free-market incentives are in place.

13. **Migrants and employers who do not comply with the new law should be punished.** Migrants who decline to register and are subsequently apprehended inside the U.S. should be punished with more than deportation. Deportation is not a disincentive. The Cornyn-Kyl bill (S. 1438) contains a good proposal along these lines: a 10-year ban on guest worker participation for migrants who do not comply with the new program.[11] Congress should also consider a lifetime prohibition on violators' applying for and receiving U.S. citizenship. The law should introduce steep penalties as well, including prison time and seizure of assets of undocumented workers and their employers. There is no justification for working outside the system, especially a system that allows free entry. The law would establish a date certain after which all migrants in the U.S. must be registered or face these penalties. The lifetime ban on the opportunity to acquire U.S. citizenship would be a strong incentive for undocumented immigrants to enter the process of documentation. Likewise, firm, consistent, enforced penalties against employers would create the proper incentives for compliance.

14. **All migrants should respect American law and traditions.** The requirement to obey all laws is not optional for new citizens and should not be optional for visitors. While we encourage and insist on the primacy of American values for those who join our workforce, we should also remember the full spectrum of values ourselves. The Statue of Liberty reminds us that we are all equal, regardless of ethnicity,

origin, or even state of wretchedness, and that America will continue to be a land of opportunity.

Conclusion

The century of globalization will see America either descend into timid isolation or affirm its openness. Throughout history, great nations have declined because they built up walls of insularity, but America has been the exception for over a century. It would be a tragedy if America were to turn toward a false sense of security just when China is ascending with openness, Western Europe is declining into isolation, and the real solution is so obvious from our own American heritage.

Stop the Muslim Migrants

Daniel Greenfield

In the following viewpoint, Daniel Greenfield alleges that many people claiming to be Syrian refugees are looking for easier lives rather than fleeing violence. He believes that Muslim terrorists and war criminals are entering Europe and the United States disguised as refugees. His opinion is that only Christian refugees should be admitted. Daniel Greenfield is a journalist who focuses on radical Islam.

As you read, consider the following questions:

1. What does this article suggests would happen if borders were closed and refugees sent back to Syria?
2. Who does Greenfield see as the real victims of the crisis?
3. Does Greenfield cite any verifiable statistics to support his claims?

The Syrian refugee crisis that the media bleats about is not a crisis. And the Syrian refugees it champions are often neither Syrians nor refugees. Fake Syrian passports are cheaper than an EU politician's virtue and easier to come by. Just about anyone who speaks enough Arabic to pass the scrutiny of a European bureaucrat can come with his two wives in tow and take a turn on the carousel of their welfare state.

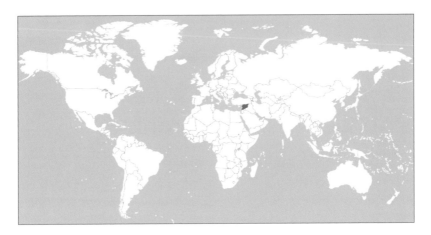

Or on our welfare state, which pays Christian and Jewish groups to bring the Muslim terrorists of tomorrow to our towns and cities. And their gratitude will be as short-lived as our budgets.

The head of a UNHCR camp called Syrian refugees "The most difficult refugees I've ever seen. In Bulgaria, they complained that there were no jobs. In Sweden, they took off their clothes to protest that it was too cold.

In Italy, Muslim African "refugees" rejected pasta and demanded food from their own countries. But the cruel Europeans who "mistreat" migrants set up a kitchen in Calais with imported spices cooked by a Michelin chef determined to give them the stir-fried rabbit and lamb meatballs they're used to. There are also mobile phone charging stations so the destitute refugees can check on their Facebook accounts.

It had to be done because the refugees in Italy were throwing rocks at police while demanding free wifi.

This is the tawdry sense of entitlement of the Syrian Muslim refugee that the media champions.

Hussein said: "We have the feeling that the aid workers are heartless." (He) lives in a trailer that cost $3,000. The air-conditioner runs with electricity he is tapping from the Italian hospital. The water for his tea is from canisters provided by UNICEF. He hasn't worked, paid or thanked anyone for any of it."

And why would he? He's entitled to it by virtue of his superiority as a Muslim and our inferiority as infidels. There is no sense of gratitude. Only constant demands as if the people who drove out their own Christians and Jews have some moral claim on the charity of the Christians and Jews of the West.

The media howls that the Syrian refugee crisis is our fault. That is a lie.

What is happening in Syria is a religious civil war fought over the same ideologies as the ones practiced by the vast majority of the refugees. This is an Islamic war fought to determine which branch of Islam will be supreme. It is not a war that started last week or last year, but 1,400 years ago.

We can't make it go away by overthrowing Assad or supporting him, by giving out candy or taking in refugees. This conflict is in the cultural DNA of Islam. It is not going anywhere.

This war is not our fault. It is their fault.

There are Christian and non-Muslim minorities who are genuine refugees, but the two Muslim sects whose militias are murdering each other are not victims, they are perpetrators. Just because Sunnis are running from a Shiite militia or Shiites from a Sunni militia right now doesn't make them victims.

The moment that their side's militia wins and begins slaughtering the other side, the oppressed will become the oppressors. Such shifts have already taken place countless times in this conflict.

The refugees aren't fleeing a dictator, they're fleeing each other while carrying the hateful ideologies that caused this bloodshed with them.

We aren't taking in people fleeing the civil war. We're taking in their civil war and giving it a good home.

The Tsarnaevs left behind their old war with the Russian infidels to begin a new phase of it against the American infidels. The children of the Syrian Muslim refugees we're taking in will be raised in a faith and a culture that will cause them to play out the same old patterns that led to the current tragedy.

There are already Syrians, Iraqis and Afghans fighting each other in Greece. Muslim migrants are murdering Christian refugees on the journey over. And this is only the beginning.

The ranks of the refugees include possible war criminals like Abu Hussein, the commander of a Free Syrian Army militia named the Falcons of the Tribe of the Prophet Mohammed, who controls portions of a UNHCR refugee camp and threatens to kill aid workers when they won't give him what he wants.

The bleeding hearts of Europe and America want to take in the cute kiddies, but they'll be getting the Husseins instead who will be running neighborhoods in London, Paris and Toronto. And then the kindly natives will notice that their daughters are coming home late and wonder what is happening to them.

Syria will happen to them. Just as Pakistan and Afghanistan happened to the British girls victimized by the Muslim sex grooming gangs in the UK. Just as Saudi Arabia happened to us on September 11.

A popular meme claims that the UK has taken in only enough refugees to fit on a subway train. My question to the meme spreaders is how would they like to be on that train, wedged between the terrorists, the sex groomers and the Sunnis and Shiites trying to reach across and throttle each other.

We are told that the Syrian refugees "stir the conscience" of the world; certainly not the Muslim world. The Saudis don't want them. Jordan and Turkey have resentfully set up refugee camps without actually offering permanent legal status to them the way that Europe, Canada and America are expected to.

What do Muslim countries know about the Syrian Civil War that we don't?

The Saudis, Jordanians and Turks have their own problems. They don't want to import the Syrian Civil War into their own borders. Only Western countries are stupid enough to do that.

The Syrian refugee crisis is a voluntary crisis. It would go away in a snap with secure borders and rapid deportations. The fake

Syrians would stay home if they knew that their fake passport wouldn't earn them a train ride to Germany's Hartz welfare state, but a memorable trip to the Syrian Civil War.

Even announcing such a policy would lead to a rapid wave of self-deportations by finicky refugees for whom Bulgarian jobs, Italian food and Swedish weather aren't good enough.

Plenty of Syrian refugees returned on their own from the Zaatari camp in Jordan, when they saw that there weren't enough treats for them. They went back to Syria from Turkey and even Europe when they didn't find life to their liking. If they were really facing death back home, they would have stayed. There were no Jews going back to Germany during the Holocaust because they couldn't find jobs in New York. Nobody goes home to a genocide. They go home because they were economic migrants, not refugees.

The crisis here is caused by the magnet of Western welfare states. Get rid of the magnet and you get rid of the crisis. Stop letting migrants who show up stay and there will be no more photogenic rafts filled with "starving" and "desperate" people who pay thousands of dollars to get to Europe and then complain about the food and the weather. Put up border fences and the "hikers" will go back home.

Keeping the doors open intensifies the crisis. It's the sympathy of the bleeding hearts that leads to dead children whose parents are willing to risk their lives for their own economic goals. The left creates the crisis and then indicts everyone else for refusing to accept its solution that would make it even worse.

The "humanitarian catastrophe" in which the migrants use their children as photogenic human shields would go away if the doors were closed to everyone except real refugees who were not part of this war. The only thing that taking in fake refugees does is attract more of them and that empowers the left which uses dead children for its power and profit at more places than just Planned Parenthood.

Slovakia has announced that it will only take in Christian refugees and that's the right thing to do. Christians are the real victims of this Muslim conflict. The vast majority of the refugees, many of whom aren't even Syrians, aren't. The rest of Europe should use Slovakia's refugee policy as a model.

Periodical and Internet Sources Bibliography

The following articles have been selected to supplement the diverse views presented in this chapter.

Mona Christophersen, "Syria's Refugees: Toward a Policy of Selective Inclusion", Global Observatory, May 16, 2016. https://theglobalobservatory.org/2016/05/syria-refugee-humanitarian-selective-inclusion/

Don Clemmer, "Bishops' Migration Chair: U.S. Should Welcome Syrian Refugees, Work For Peace", United States Conference of Catholic Bishops, November 17, 2015. http://www.usccb.org/news/2015/15-157.cfm

Leo Hohmann, "So It Begins Here", WorldNetDaily, February 2, 2016. http://www.wnd.com/2016/02/so-it-begins-here-u-s-city-overrun-with-criminal-refugees/

Arsla Jawaid, "How the Exclusion of Muslims Could Help Extremists", Global Observatory, February 3, 2017. https://theglobalobservatory.org/2017/02/trump-immigration-refugee-muslim-ban-exclusion/

Howard Johnson and Tobias Bräuer, "Migrant Crisis: Changing attitudes of a German city", BBC News. April 28, 2016. http://www.bbc.com/news/world-europe-36148418

"Migration and Health: key issues", World Health Organization. http://www.euro.who.int/en/health-topics/health-determinants/migration-and-health/migrant-health-in-the-european-region/migration-and-health-key-issues

"Refugee Health Guidelines", Centers For Disease Control And Prevention. Vttps://www.cdc.gov/immigrantrefugeehealth/guidelines/refugee-guidelines.html

Paul Solman, "What's the Economic Impact of Refugees in America?" PBS News Hour, April 7, 2016. http://www.pbs.org/newshour/making-sense/whats-the-economic-impact-of-refugees-in-america/

United Nations, "UN Summit for Refugees and Migrants: What's Next?" United Nations. http://refugeesmigrants.un.org/infographics

United Nations, "New York Declaration for Refugees and Migrants," United Nations, October 3, 2016. http://www.un.org/en/

development/ desa/population/migration/ generalassembly/ docs/A_RES_71_1_E.pdf

Alan B West, "Coming to America soon: You won't believe what Muslim refugees are doing now…", January 24, 2016. http://www. allenbwest.com/analytical-economist/flashback-germany-admits-new-huge-problem-from-refugee-crisis

CHAPTER 4

| Responses to
Migration

Europe's Successes and Failures in Handling the Refugee Crisis

Ian Lesser, Astrid Ziebarth, Alexandra de Hoop Scheffer, Michal Baranowski, Ivan Vejvoda, Gordana Delic, and Ozgur Unluhisarcikli

In the following viewpoint, experts from the German Marshall Fund (GMF) claim that the United States is affected by the refugee crisis in Europe. They suggest that the US would benefit from successful refugee integration by making Europe more like the US and by reducing the rise of right-wing elements. The authors look at how specific European countries have reacted to Syrian refugees, both politically and socially, and address some large-scale issues that the different countries will need to tackle in order to successfully integrate the large number of incoming refugees. The German Marshall Fund (GMF) is a nonpartisan American public policy think tank dedicated to promoting cooperation between North America and Europe.

As you read, consider the following questions:

1. How might the United States benefit if Europe successfully integrates refugees from the Middle East?
2. What is the approximate length of the border that Europe has to control if it wants to control the entrance of refugees?

"The Refugee Crisis: Perspectives from Across Europe and the Atlantic", by Ian Lesser, Astrid Ziebarth, Alexandra de Hoop Scheffer, Michal Baranowski, Ivan Vejvoda, Gordana Delic, and Ozgur Unluhisarcikli from The German Marshall Fund of the United States, September 11, 2015. Reprinted by permission. This was originally published by the German Marshall Fund of the United States gmfus.org.

3. How are Balkan migrants viewed as different from Syrian refugees?

I n this brief, GMF experts from across Europe examine the scope of the crisis and the different national reactions to it in France, Germany, Poland, Serbia, and Turkey — with the transatlantic view offered by the organization's Brussels office. The authors outline the diverse political challenges faced by these governments that have so far hindered a more pragmatic humanitarian response to the crisis.

Transatlantic Stakes in Europe's Migration Crisis

Ian Lesser, Executive Director, Transatlantic
Center and Brussels Office

The United States is not an uninterested bystander in Europe's refugee crisis. If mishandled, the mounting flow of refugees and economic migrants from Europe's chaotic periphery will pose multiple challenges to U.S. interests and could prove a divisive element in transatlantic relations.

First, in the view of many Europeans, the United States is already implicated in the current crisis. In Brussels, it is not uncommon to hear that today's unprecedented refugee flows are the direct result of failed strategy toward Afghanistan, Iraq, Syria, and the Middle East as a whole. For those European political elites and publics who have been critical of U.S. policy in these areas, the flow of people from crisis-torn countries is increasingly seen as a new and tragic consequence of the inability to consolidate security after interventions, or in the case of Syria, the failure to intervene. Many Americans might agree with elements of this argument. But European policies have also failed to produce stability on Europe's southern periphery, and in the case of Libya, where the collapse of sovereignty has facilitated the trafficking in refugees and economic migrants, Europe is chiefly responsible.

Second, the United States cannot fail to be concerned about the consequences of a protracted migration crisis for the future of Europe. Successful integration of refugees from Syria and elsewhere, and a Europe more comfortable with multiculturalism, would more closely resemble the United States and could be a force for transatlantic convergence. By contrast, social tensions and a strident debate about borders, immigration, and European identity will bolster right-wing populists. These movements are already on the rise in Europe, and populists and nationalists — generally anti-American — will spell trouble for transatlantic relations. A closed and intolerant Europe will be a very uncomfortable partner for the United States. More broadly, deep divisions within the EU over migration and asylum policy, potentially far more significant than differences over the Greek debt crisis or Russia, could pose a grave challenge to the future of the EU itself. If we accept that the United States is a key stakeholder in a more concerted and active EU, the risks to U.S. interests are clear.

Finally, a spiraling migration crisis across Europe's 3,000-mile border in the Mediterranean (closer to 4,000 if Turkey's borders are included) will add to the problems already facing NATO. U.S. and European allies are only beginning to grapple with security risks emanating from the south. The collapse of regimes and the spread of chaotic conditions that have encouraged the rise of the self-proclaimed Islamic State group (ISIS) have also created a vast human security crisis. This extraordinary instability, at the intersection of Europe and the Middle East, could characterize the strategic environment on Europe's periphery for the foreseeable future. If so, the United States' interests and engagement in North Africa, the Middle East, and even South Asia may be seen increasingly through the lens of European stability.

Europe's migration problem is set to become a more central part of the United States' transatlantic calculus. By most measures, the United States is one of the largest recipients of asylum seekers on a global basis — registering 121,000 claims last year and resettling a further 50,000. But given that it is receiving fewer claims than Germany in this current crisis, this reality may not impress European leaders and publics. The announcement from the administration of U.S. President Barack Obama that it is prepared to admit up to 10,000 Syrian refugees is a useful start. Defense spending should not be the only issue on the burden-sharing agenda across the Atlantic, and U.S. assistance on this front might help ease the contentious political debate on asylum within the EU. The clock is ticking on an effective response from Brussels, and the United States has a direct stake in the outcome.

Germany: Welcoming but with Limits

Astrid Ziebarth, Migration Fellow, Europe Program

Germany has been at the forefront of the reception of refugees and migrants and is now feeling the strain that countries like Italy and Greece have felt for a long time. Last year, about 200,000 people filed for asylum in Germany overall. By just July of this year, 218,000 people had filed and official estimates for the whole year have been raised to as many as 800,000, if not a million. The top three countries of origin overall in 2015 (statistics from July) are Syria (44,000), Kosovo (33,000), and Albania (30,000). With Germany expecting to take up between 800,000 and 1 million people, it is one of the main countries to push for a quota system among EU member states that would relocate and redistribute 160,000 people currently in Italy, Greece, and Hungary. The number of people coming to Germany increased substantially in September, especially after the dramatic weekend of September 5-6, when Germany decided to take in refugees stranded in Hungary. German Chancellor Angela Merkel received both praise and criticism for this decision, within and outside Germany. Critics said that this measure, even though it was originally deemed a one-time event, encouraged people to start moving toward Europe, and Germany in particular. Others praised her humanity in this situation. Both assessments are correct.

Yes, reinstalling temporary border controls over the weekend of September 12-13 can be seen as a direct consequence of Germans openness. The pictures of friendly Germans welcoming refugees at train stations and helping them get situated and tabloids printing four-page special inserts in Arabic to help with the orientation for refugees in Berlin certainly did go around the world and even led some commentators to dub Germany a "hippie nation." But to say that Merkel has flip-flopped on the issue by instating border controls is not correct. She has defended her stance that there is a right to asylum in Germany, and that those that have a rightful claim will be able to stay. She always made it clear that those who do not have a rightful claim — mostly from the Western Balkans — will be sent home and banned from re-entering Germany.

However, she simply could no longer ignore the calls of German mayors and state governors from across the political spectrum who warned about a collapse of the system and asked for breathing space; the numbers of people entering Germany had increased too quickly. They needed a signal that she heard their concerns. These days, even a few hours of breathing space can mean a lot. It can mean beds that can be organized, housing that can be found, and volunteers that can be recruited.

Those that criticize her now should have to answer the question of what alternatives she would have really had when the situation worsened and people started to march on the highways toward Germany from the Budapest train station. At that point, just three days after the world was shocked by the picture of drowned 3-year-old Aylan Kurdi, an immediate decision needed to be taken, and nations all around the globe had to hold up a mirror and question their stance on this humanitarian crisis. Reacting to criticism that the open-door policy had been a mistake, Merkel used an unusually direct tone: "Seriously, if we have to start apologizing now that we show a friendly face in emergency situations, then this is not my country." She could have tried to set up border controls as quickly as possible at that point, and yes, this may have kept law and order and a broken Dublin system in place. It would have probably also led to fingers pointed at the coldhearted Germans from around the world. But Angela Merkel made a decision, one that will make it into the history books, for better or for worse.

Viewing a Crisis as an Opportunity

The Arab Spring marked for Italy the start of a migration emergency that has since been worsened by developments in Syria and Iraq, and most of all in Libya. Hundreds of thousands of people have been leaving Libya by sea to reach Italy, and of these several thousands have lost their lives.

[…]

No less than four different Italian governments opted for different approaches; some blamed the EU for its inefficiency and failure to respond to Italy's calls for assistance, and others looked for buffer solutions while trying to convince their EU partners that the migrant crisis was not just a passing phenomenon but a structural fact.

Meanwhile, other EU countries blame Italy for having disregarded existing agreements concerning economic migrants who should be returned to their own country, and asylum-seekers who need to be assessed by the EU country they first entered.

Italy's inability to do this has quickly encouraged migrants to quit Italian refugee centres and head for their real destinations in France, Germany or Sweden. This has generated border tensions, especially with France.

The drowning tragedies that shocked public opinion in Italy saw the launch in autumn 2013 of the Mare Nostrum patrol mission in Libyan territorial waters to rescue migrants aboard unsafe ships. A year later, Mare Nostrum was replaced by the European Triton mission as part of the Frontex programme for securing the EU's external borders.

The Italian argument that all this is a European issue, not a national one, has been reinforced by the much greater number of migrants reaching not only Italy but also Greece. The result has been the European Commission's plan for sharing the burden among all 28 EU states. But Italy, like others, still needs to manage immigration not just as an emergency but as a structural reality. And it also needs to accept the idea that immigration, even the economic kind, can be a development opportunity for countries with an aging and shrinking population.

"How Italy is still struggling with the refugee crisis," by Giampiero Gramaglia, Europe's World, October 26, 2015.

For a brief time, she reminded us that in emergency situations, you help out as best as you can.

Refugees and Migration: A Tricky Issue in France

Alexandra de Hoop Scheffer, Senior Transatlantic Fellow, and Director, Paris Office

French President François Hollande's recent decision to take in 24,000 refugees over the next two years as part of a Europe-wide quota plan is an about-face for France, after having said in May that quotas were "out of the question." France has been reluctant to open its doors to migrants and refugees, but the government shifted position after Berlin's push for a permanent and mandatory mechanism for distributing refugees across the EU.

The refugee crisis is testing intra-European solidarity and pushing France and Germany to advance joint responsibility-sharing measures at the European level, despite diverging national perceptions. But France is unlikely to offer the same kind of welcome Germany has given refugees, for several reasons.

Migration remains a very tricky issue in France, where record high levels of unemployment and fear of terrorism have fueled anti-immigration sentiment. Home to Europe's largest Muslim population, France is in the middle of an "identity crisis." The recent "migrant crisis" of Calais, which monopolized French media attention during the summer, has already highlighted society's sensitivity to the issue. Last January's terrorist attacks in Paris also help explain French fears. According to an opinion poll published by Le Parisien, 56 percent of French people interviewed believed that terrorists may be among the thousands of refugees heading into Europe, a fear that Germans do not share. The same poll revealed that 55 percent of French people surveyed were opposed to an easing of rules for asylum seekers, including for Syrians fleeing civil war.

It is this kind of fear and skepticism that Marine Le Pen's far-right Front National has helped to stoke in recent months. A number of French local authorities (mostly from the Front National and some conservatives from Les Républicains) oppose welcoming refugees in their cities, mostly for political and sometimes religious reasons (refusal to host Muslims). They also want more financial support from the government if they are to host additional refugees. At the same time, cities around France have also seen pro-refugee demonstrations, like in Nantes where more than 1,200 took to the streets to support welcoming refugees. More than a dozen towns, mostly with left-wing mayors, have offered to take in Syrians.

The refugee crisis has sparked fierce debate and profound divisions in France, with Le Pen leading opposition to opening the borders. Ex-president Nicolas Sarkozy, leader of the conservative opposition Les Républicains, called for detention camps to be set up in neighboring countries under EU control to filter migrants and refugees before they crossed the Mediterranean. He also repeated past calls for an end to the EU's Schengen zone of open border travel. In this context, Hollande sought to rally the public's support by focusing on the international dimensions of the migration crisis, and announced his resolve to get more involved militarily to combat what he considers to be the root of the problem: ISIS. This decision is broadly endorsed by the French people and the political class. The same survey, conducted by the Odoxa polling institute, said 61 percent were in favor of France taking part in a coalition sending ground troops to Syria to fight ISIS.

Hollande also joined with Angela Merkel in drafting a Joint Letter to European Leaders on September 3, promoting common European asylum laws, a list of "safe countries of origin," and calling for an increase of the European aid to Turkey, Lebanon, and Jordan in their efforts to welcome refugees.

Hollande said several factors — notably the foiled terrorist attack on a Paris-bound train in August and the shocking photo of the body of three-year-old Ayland Kurdi on a Turkish beach — influenced his decisions to heighten engagement in Syria and take in more refugees. However, France's poor economic performance, the mood of anxiety following the Charlie Hebdo attacks, and the influence of the far-right on the public and political debate, will continue to make migration a tricky issue for any French government. Only true political leadership and courage could help turn the tide.

Poland's Shifting Stand

Michał Baranowski, Director, Warsaw Office

For the past months, Poland has not been seen as part of the solution to the migration crisis in Europe. However, Polish Prime Minister Ewa Kopacz this week signaled a greater flexibility and willingness to contribute. "Now the situation is much more serious — it's a real humanitarian crisis, therefore we are considering a very significant increase in our engagement," she said on September 9.[1]

To date, Poland had agreed to accept around 2,000 asylum seekers. But according to the plan of the European Commission Jean-Claude Juncker presented in early September, Poland would have to accept over 11,000 refugees. So far, very few political refugees have made their way to Poland — this year Poland accepted only 250 asylum seekers. But this might change rapidly if the migration routes change, which could happen if Hungary completes its border fence. There is also a legitimate concern over a possible flow of refugees from Ukraine due to the conflict with Russia. Though the number of political refugees is very small, there are an estimated 300,000 to 400,000 Ukrainians in Poland, including Ukrainians who received permits for short-term work and those working in the black market.

Domestically, the debate over migration could not come at worse time for the current government, led by Platforma Obywatelska. Poland will hold parliamentary elections on October 25, which the main opposition party, the right-wing Law and Justice (PiS), is poised to win. Migration is a new, difficult, and unpopular issue in Polish politics. The government finds itself between a rock and a hard place, with pressure from Brussels and Berlin to open up its borders, and an opposition that vehemently criticizes any move to cave to Europe and let in refugees. The election dynamics will make it hard for the government to join the European consensus. But the latest change of heart by Kopacz suggests that she decided to defuse the political bomb with the election still more than a month out, rather than facing an embarrassing defeat in the European Council, which will vote on the migration crisis solution right before the October elections. There is a clear understanding in Poland that opposing a common solution to the refugee crisis would damage Poland's standing in the EU. Recently, the prime minister warned against a "breakdown of European solidarity" and asked what would happen if Poland needs to ask its European partners for solidarity in dealing with challenges coming from the east.

The refugee and migration crisis has led to soul searching in Poland, as in the rest of Europe. The crisis has provoked a deeply emotional national debate not only among politicians, but also artists, writers, and the general public. It is a moral issue, it is an economic issue, it is a cultural and identity issue, and finally it is an issue of Poland's place in Europe. Public opinion is divided, but also shifting. A majority of Polish respondents (53 percent) believes that Poland has a moral duty to accept migrants, while 44 percent disagrees with this assessment. Twenty-two percent of Poles think that their country should not accept any refugees at all. Only 9 percent believe that Poland should take more than 10,000, as Juncker suggested this week.

In the period before the parliamentary elections, the Polish government will attempt to balance between demands from its European partners and the pressure of the opposition. The government will push back on the compulsory quota — Kopacz stated that "Poland wants to have a control over who and how many people come."

Poland, as well as other Central and Eastern European countries, will need not only political pressure, but also concrete knowledge and logistical assistance in order to take on a larger refugee population. Poland only has the infrastructure in place to deal with 2,000-3,000 refugees. It also has little experience in dealing with migration from distant places, and even less with integrating these migrants or refugees into its still ethnically and religiously homogenous society.

The issue of migration is with us to stay. A politically sustainable solution will have to account for differences among EU member states, but also to create mechanism to turn the migration crisis into a boon for an aging and shrinking Europe.

The Balkan Route and its Implications for the EU

Ivan Vejvoda, Senior Vice President for Programs

The thousands of migrants/refugees entering the European Union via Greece want to stay within the EU but in its north, in Germany or Scandinavia. To do this, they have to pass through the inner courtyard of geographic and political Europe: the Balkans. And the route takes them through states that are aspiring candidates for full membership in the EU, principally Macedonia and Serbia.

The next entry point into a full member state of the EU, after passing through those two countries, is Hungary. Its government, going against the grain of other EU member states and core values of the Union, has unilaterally built a barrier along its 175 kilometer-long border with Serbia, a 4 meter-high barb-wired "fence" that will allegedly be backed up by a planned stronger second barrier. Hungarian police have used tear gas and water cannons against refugees protesting the closing of the border. Orban has also announced plans to erect fences on Hungary's borders to Romania and Croatia, which is already receiving a lot of the redirected refugees passing through Serbia.

Hungary is an exception to the rule in the way Europe's countries are reacting to the inflow of migrants and refugees. Four thousand people were waiting to cross the Macedonian border into Serbia this past Thursday, while about 3,000, mostly Syrians, are arriving daily on the island of Lesbos before heading for the Greek mainland, according to Greek police. From there, they too will likely traverse the Balkan route.

On Friday, the Bulgarian and Serbian prime ministers spoke on the phone to coordinate responses and practical measures, within an EU framework, and agreed to a three-way meeting with their Romanian counterpart in the latter part of the month. All three, as have other European leaders, have opposed the idea of building new walls in Europe and seek other ways to address the wave of mostly transitioning migrants.

This crisis has raised a number of issues for the region and its relations with the EU. For the Balkan region especially, there is the question of how non-member states can partake in a joint and coordinated EU response. At the Vienna EU-Balkan Summit on August 27, the day that the infamous truck with bodies of 71 migrants was discovered on a highway near Vienna, there was a clear statement that "strengthened cooperation and additional support" was needed in the effort to address the challenge.

Addressing issues of border control, cross-border crime fighting, counter-terrorism, and the migration challenge requires a fully coordinated approach of EU and non-EU member states. Only such an approach can produce minimally satisfactory results.

Serbia Struggles Admirably to Assist Refugees

Gordana Delic, Director, Balkan Trust for Democracy and Belgrade Office

Serbia is situated along the preferred route through the Western Balkans for refugees/migrants from the Middle East and Asia on their way to asylum in Europe. The majority are from Syria, Afghanistan, and Iraq. According to UNHCR data, the number of those registered as intention to seek asylum averaged 1,290 people per day in Serbia. By September 7, a total of 112,630 persons were registered in 2015, but only 500 requested asylum. The rest passed through Serbia and crossed into Hungary.

Serbia has been doing a good job providing humanitarian assistance and registration documents to the refugees/migrants. A One-Stop Center and a Refugee Aid Point (RAP) have been opened close to the Macedonian border where refugees/migrants are provided with the appropriate documents, food, emergency medical care, and a place to rest. A third temporary reception center was opened in August close to Serbian-Hungarian border. In central Belgrade, about 1,000 to 2,000 refuges/migrants are camping in a park near the main bus station. Usually they stay 24 to 48 hours, and they receive aid from government institutions, international organizations, NGOs, and volunteers.

Before winter, Serbia will have to create more accommodation, primarily in Belgrade, so it is a positive development that Serbian Prime Minister Aleksandar Vučić recently announced that the government plans to build a temporary reception center in the city. Vučić said "Serbia can't close its eyes like others in Europe have. Refugees are safe and welcome here. Some will stay, although we know they want to go to more developed countries. If they want to stay, we have no problem. These are good, hard-working people." At Serbia's border to Hungary, there have been clashes, protests, and hunger strikes by refugees since Hungary closed off its side. But Serbia is continuing to provide support, and the refugees have already begun to be rerouted to Croatia.

Serbian society has responded positively to this difficult situation. Even the Serbian Orthodox Church has called on the public to help migrants. A right-wing politician's suggestion to build a wall at Serbia's border with Macedonia was immediately dismissed by both government and opposition.

An emergency plan to respond to the current migration crisis was adopted last week. It is not yet publicly available but apparently the plan foresees two new directions of refugee/migrant movement: toward Romania and toward Croatia. New locations for accommodation of refugees/migrants will be established on these routes. However, Serbia is highlighting both the need for a joint response of all EU countries to this situation and its readiness to follow the EU approach. The government of Serbia is also asking the European Union and the international community for financial assistance.

Juncker has called for reform of disparate immigration policies in the EU and for European states to accept binding quotas to resettle 160,000 refugees. But there are still no concrete proposals regarding the role and responsibilities of countries outside of the EU, like Serbia, related to "burden sharing" of refugees/ migrants processing.

Before winter, the Serbian government, in cooperation with governments in the region, the EU, and relevant international actors should define following mid-term solutions:

- First, we need a common definition of the status of the refugees (who is a refugee, and who is a migrant), and a uniform regional approach to their rights and benefits.

- Second, in cooperation with the EU and regional governments, Serbia too, should take part in the quota system, and take on a certain number of refugees. In that context, Serbia will have to develop integration policies in cooperation with civil society and international actors.

- Finally, we should establish better facilities near borders that could assess the persons on the move and initiate the appropriate procedures such as asylum, readmission, victims of trafficking, and a procedure for vulnerable groups.

Europe's Small Taste of Turkey's Refugee Crisis

Özgür Ünlühisarcıklı, Director, *Ankara Office*

The Syrian refugee crisis has accelerated Turkey's already ongoing transition from a country of emigration to a transit and host country. With a 911-kilometer land border with Syria and an open border policy toward refugees from its southern neighbor, the official number of Syrian refugees Turkey hosts has reached 1.7 million as of September 2015;[2] unofficial figures go as high as 2 million. Two-hundred-sixty thousand of these refugees live in 25 "temporary protection centers" located in ten cities across Turkey; the others have chosen to live outside these centers. Turkey has spent $5.6 billion on Syrian refugees since the beginning of the crisis.

In addition to hosting these refugees, Turkey is also a transit country for most of the refugees heading to the EU. Transit flows of Syrian refugees through Turkey to Europe have led to public and political debates on burden sharing and humanitarian issues. The picture of three-year-old Aylan Kurdi, found lying dead on a beach after the boat in which his family was trying to get to the Greek island of Chios capsized, caused international sorrow. French President François Hollande phoned Turkish President Recep Tayyip Erdoğan and some European leaders after the images of Kurdi emerged in the world media and said that "the picture must be a reminder of the world's responsibility regarding refugees."

In an article published by the Guardian on September 9, 2015, Prime Minister Ahmet Davutoğlu said "Turkey, traditionally a transit country for irregular migration, is now also a top destination. The Turkish people have made huge sacrifices in hosting more than 2 million Syrians and Iraqis. By so doing, we have damped the mass influx to the EU and effectively become a buffer between chaos and Europe. Meanwhile, EU member states account for ridiculously low shares in the global resettlement rates."

The Syrian refugee crisis has also accelerated legal and institutional reforms regarding migration: a law on foreigners and international protection that brings Turkey in line with international standards was adopted in April 2013 and a temporary protection regulation to create a system to provide Syrian refugees with satisfactory protection and humanitarian assistance was enacted in October 2014.

The Turkish public is not overwhelmingly positive about the refugees. According to Transatlantic Trends Survey 2014 findings, 77 percent of Turks surveyed were worried about refugees and 66 percent wanted more restrictive refugee policies. However, at least for the moment, the issue is not being politicized and the opposition parties have not made a big issue out of it either. With the exception of some isolated incidents, there has not been a significant backlash against the refugees.

While Europe is facing the dramatic consequences of the Syrian refugee crisis this year, Turkey has been quietly adapting since the beginning of the conflict in Syria. However ,Turkey still has room for improvement and there are ways Europe can help. Turkey needs to decide whether the Syrians on its soil are guests, as they are officially called, or future citizens, which may be the hard truth. The answer to this question would play a large role in determining the appropriate set of policies. European countries have an interest in helping Turkey deal with this crisis, including financially. The approximately $400 million that the international community has so far provided to help the refugees in Turkey falls short of lightening Ankara's almost $6 billion burden. Without more help, Europe is bound to see an even greater number of refugees traveling through Turkey to its borders and beyond.

[…]

EU-Turkey Agreement Could Fail Legally and Logistically

Elizabeth Collett

In the following viewpoint, Elizabeth Collett examines the agreement between the European Union and Turkey to handle migrants. She questions whether the agreement is legal and workable, suggesting that the logistical challenges are even more serious than the legal ones. At worst, opportunities will be squandered and Europe will only create a different version of the crisis. Conditions for refugees could worsen and trouble spots moved to new areas. The Migration Policy Institute (MPI) is a nonpartisan think tank based in Washington DC. Elizabeth Collett is the Founding Director of MPI Europe, focused on European migration and immigrant integration policy.

As you read, consider the following questions:

1. What is the goal of the EU-Turkey agreement?
2. What is meant by a "safe third country"?
3. What international laws affect the legality of returning refugees to their home country?

As European governments rapidly turn their attention to the implementation of the EU-Turkey agreement, observers have raised serious questions regarding whether the deal itself is legal, and more importantly, if it will even work. The 28 EU heads of state forged the March 18 deal with Turkey with their backs

"The Paradox of the EU-Turkey Refugee Deal," by Elizabeth Collett, Migration Policy Institute, March 2016. Reprinted by permission.

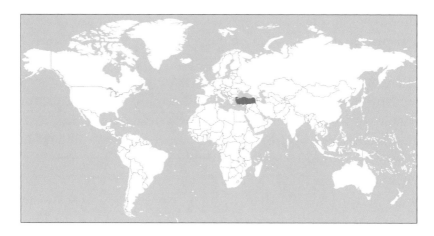

seemingly against the wall, and in an atmosphere of palpable panic. At its core, the agreement aims to address the overwhelming flow of smuggled migrants and asylum seekers traveling across the Aegean from Turkey to the Greek islands by allowing Greece to return to Turkey "all new irregular migrants" arriving after March 20. In exchange, EU Member States will increase resettlement of Syrian refugees residing in Turkey, accelerate visa liberalization for Turkish nationals, and boost existing financial support for Turkey's refugee population.

For leaders the objective was clear: to find a way to prevent unchecked arrivals into the European Union. The fact that a group of 28 states with increasingly divergent interests was able to find consensus speaks to the level of concern that leaders have for their own domestic political futures in a context of rising populism.

However, the deal has also unveiled a paradox for a European Union that has spent several decades preaching its own high asylum standards to neighboring countries. To achieve its self-imposed goal—a significant reduction in arrivals and an increase in returns to Turkey—policymakers will have to drastically cut legal corners, potentially violating EU law on issues such as detention and the right to appeal. But if governments execute the agreement in conformity with international and European legal frameworks, few arrivals are likely to be returned, and the agreement risks becoming the latest in a long series of undelivered promises to exasperated publics for whom the complex legal conundrums of implementation are both meaningless and irrelevant.

While the former route is deeply tempting for policymakers, undermining Europe's human-rights commitments in such a visible way may prove even more costly in the long-term than the current chaos in Greece. Leaders are clearly aware of the risk. In the days leading up to the final agreement, the European Union back-pedaled significantly from rhetoric about creating "a large-scale mechanism to ship back irregular migrants" to an assessment process respecting the asylum rights of each individual reaching Greece. A strong backlash from refugee and other human-rights organizations confirmed this, including the United Nations High Commissioner for Refugees (UNHCR) which highlighted long-standing international prohibitions on collective expulsion, or "blanket returns." But the speed and unchartered nature of the implementation may mean rules are set aside in favor of expediency.

Thus, governments are taking a bet that the "messaging" of the EU-Turkey agreement, rather than its implementation, will suffice to deter arrivals without having to test its legality or viability in practice.

Can Anyone be Returned?

EU law currently allows for returns under two circumstances. First, individuals who do not apply or do not qualify for asylum are considered "irregular migrants" and are eligible to be returned to Turkey under an existing readmission agreement with Greece (pending the implementation in June 2016 of a readmission agreement between the European Union and Turkey). Second, individuals who submit asylum claims but are determined to have arrived from a country where they had or could have claimed protection (a "safe third country" or "first country of asylum," the EU criteria for which include the right to nonrefoulement and the ability to both request and receive protection) are considered inadmissible to the European Union and eligible for return.

Whether Turkey truly meets the criteria to be designated a safe country, as it has been under the deal, remains in question.

A look at both the profile of recent arrivals in Greece, and the substantive protection currently available in Turkey, suggests the promised individual asylum assessments will weed out only a small proportion for return as irregular migrants, suggesting the rest will fall under the "safe third country" or "first country of asylum" categories. In February 2016 alone, more than 57,000 migrants arrived on the Greek islands; 52 percent were Syrian nationals, while a further 41 percent were Afghan and Iraqi nationals (25 and 16 percent, respectively). All three populations include those with significant protection needs, but it remains unclear whether Turkey has sufficient safeguards in place (in principle and in practice) to meet these needs to EU standards. Ensuring all returns are legal according to EU law and the 1951 Refugee Convention would thus likely lead to very few being returned.

The current protection regime in Turkey can be broadly broken down into two categories: Syrian nationals, who are given temporary protection status (with limited rights including regulated access to the labor market), and everyone else, who has a right to international protection based on the Law on Foreigners and International Protection passed in 2014 (though this stops short of full refugee status). Perhaps more troublingly, the framework for providing such protection still exists primarily on paper rather than in practice. At the end of February 2016, Turkey's caseload of asylum seekers remained more than 200,000, with just 38,595 having received protection: it will take time for the Turkish system to scale-up sufficiently to address this backlog, especially as the responsible agency is also scrambling to meet other deliverables created by the EU-Turkey deal, such as visa liberalization. This makes real access to protection for additional returnees—particularly non-Syrians—under the current EU-Turkey deal a distant prospect, and Greece would struggle to justify such returns.

The Turkish government, however, has stated that it sees its current protection framework, at least on paper, as sufficient and pushed back hard against the idea of further reform, including the full adoption of the Geneva Convention.

With respect to the Syrian population itself, nearly half of those taking the journey do so in order to join family members already residing in Europe, according to interviews conducted by UNHCR in February. Even with the EU-Turkey deal in place, asylum claims made in Greece still have to be considered according to the existing Dublin Regulation, suggesting that those with valid and verified family connections would be transferred to the appropriate EU Member State to complete asylum procedures rather than be returned to Turkey. In the wake of the March 18 summit, EU officials suggested the legal basis of returns of potential candidates for family reunification was still to be determined. Add to this the challenges of returning any children—who comprised 40 percent of all arrivals to Greece in February—given current reception conditions for minors in Turkey, and the prospects of returning significant numbers in the short-term under the current agreement look remote.

Some argue these challenges are minor, not least because the vast majority of those arriving in Greece, so far, have not filed asylum claims there—1,470 filed in February, or 2.5 percent of arrivals—with many hoping to move on throughout the European Union. However, the increased prospect of return to Turkey and the closure of the Western Balkans route may well change that dynamic. In addition, security concerns—notably terrorist attacks in Paris and Brussels—have shifted policy goals toward effective identification, registration, and management of those who are arriving, and not just on meeting protection needs.

Logistical Challenges

The challenges of meeting legal standards for the return of asylum seekers pales in comparison to the logistical challenge that has now been handed to the Greek government, in addressing both asylum and security imperatives. First, the government will need to

Large-Scale "Returns" of Syrians in Turkey

New research carried out by [Amnesty International] in Turkey's southern border provinces suggests that Turkish authorities have been rounding up and expelling groups of around 100 Syrian men, women and children to Syria on a near-daily basis since mid-January. Over three days last week, Amnesty International researchers gathered multiple testimonies of large-scale returns from Hatay province, confirming a practice that is an open secret in the region.

All forced returns to Syria are illegal under Turkish, EU and international law.

"In their desperation to seal their borders, EU leaders have willfully ignored the simplest of facts: Turkey is not a safe country for Syrian refugees and is getting less safe by the day," said John Dalhuisen, Amnesty International's Director for Europe and Central Asia.

"The large-scale returns of Syrian refugees we have documented highlight the fatal flaws in the EU-Turkey deal. It is a deal that can only be implemented with the hardest of hearts and a blithe disregard for international law."

The EU-Turkey deal paves the way for the immediate return to Turkey of Syrian refugees arriving on the Greek islands, on the grounds that it is safe country of asylum. EU officials have expressed the hope that returns could start as of Monday 4 April.

The EU's extended courting of Turkey that preceded the deal has already had disastrous knock-on effects on Turkey's own policies towards Syrian refugees.

"Far from pressuring Turkey to improve the protection it offers Syrian refugees, the EU is in fact incentivizing the opposite," said John Dalhuisen.

"It seems highly likely that Turkey has returned several thousand refugees to Syria in the last seven to nine weeks. If the agreement proceeds as planned, there is a very real risk that some of those the EU sends back to Turkey will suffer the same fate."

"Turkey: Illegal Mass Returns Of Syrian Refugees Expose Fatal Flaws In EU-Turkey Deal,"
Amnesty International, April 1, 2016.

put new legislation in place to allow for case-by-case assessments and appeals of those assessments, and to facilitate returns. This includes the prospect of judges from other EU Member States hearing appeals on the islands under Greek jurisdiction, while it is not clear Greek legislation currently allows for this.

Second, getting those judges, and other officials to the islands to effect the process will prove challenging for overstretched national administrations loathe to lose their personnel while their own asylum backlogs remain high. If Europe learned one thing during 2015, it is that pledges of officers and equipment do not materialize immediately, not least because bureaucracies take time to process transfers of human resources. Deals made in Brussels are quickly forgotten in national capitals.

In addition, building systems takes time: the EU registration hotspots in Greece took more than six months to materialize, due both to an absence of pre-existing infrastructure and a lackluster response from an exhausted Greek government. The process also revealed significant loopholes and information gaps in terms of registration and identification.

Finally, the transformation of hotspots into detention centers not only poses a logistical challenge, but also risks losing essential practical support from international and nongovernmental organizations. UNHCR, the International Rescue Committee (IRC), and Save the Children, among others, have all withdrawn services out of concern for the conditions and rights violations that will ensue. Without their support, the process loses both legitimacy and resources.

This, in turn, raises a more significant question about the evident ad hoc implementation of the EU-Turkey deal. Much of the process is being worked out on the ground by officials who are still unclear about the legal ramifications of their decisions. This may be deliberate: to increase the numbers returned, policymakers may have to feign a reality that does not currently exist, not just with regard to conditions in Turkey, but also with respect to offering arrivals a real and informed opportunity to make an asylum claim.

In doing so EU leaders would be making a calculated risk. It will take time for a case to reach either the Court of Justice of the European Union (CJEU) or the European Court of Human Rights

(ECtHR) to find the processes unlawful. The scheme has already been declared "extraordinary" and "temporary," and individuals summarily returned are unlikely to have legal recourse. The temporariness is also a political reality—should visa liberalization not materialize at the end of June, the European Union will be less likely to find a willing partner in Turkey. Thus the scheme has its own built-in detonator, but one with brutal consequences for those arrivals who are caught up in the meantime.

Looking Down the Road

The agreement's broader implications are likely too politically remote to seem real to policymakers under pressure. Much has been made of the likelihood that smugglers will diversify and adapt, and that the drivers impelling movement are not diminishing. Cessation of the en masse smuggling route across the Aegean may also push up prices for other paths, diminishing demand, while increasing danger. Leaders may accomplish their goal of reducing arrival numbers in Greece, but find themselves experiencing déjà vu. In investing huge political capital towards such a localized area, there is a reasonable risk that, within a year, Europe will have come full circle, with renewed flows across the more dangerous route across the Central Mediterranean. Ironically, one of the premises behind shutting down the Libya route in 2015 was to reduce the deeply damaging danger and death, and confine mixed flows to the less risky routes across the Eastern Mediterranean.

The reality is that EU leaders left themselves too little time to do many of the things that could have avoided such drastic deal-making with Turkey, whether offering greater assistance in countries of first asylum, or fully supporting the development of the asylum system in Greece. The opportunity to convince Turkey to develop a full protection system was lost in the exigencies of the summit negotiations, though there remains an opening to significantly bolster Greece's ability to receive, register, and process claims. The opportunity also exists to pilot a new idea that has emerged from this deal: the concept of a collaborative, EU-led fast-track assessment system that can operate at the European Union's external borders. Such a system, composed of competent adjudicators and integrating robust, early legal advice for applicants, might actually serve both the protection goal—offering asylum seekers a quick and credible assessment of their claim—as well as the migration management goal, by swiftly disaggregating the viability of claims and effecting legitimate returns. However, the haphazard implementation approaches of the last year suggest this opportunity too will be squandered, in a context where detail has become anathema to politics.

Displacing the Problem

The idea of returns coupled with large-scale resettlement is beguiling and, from a distance, charmingly simple. But policymakers have viewed the EU-Turkey deal through the lens of the last six months, amplified by concerns over Schengen, rather than the longer scope of the last (and next) five years. The complex and ever-shifting dynamics of migration flows, coupled with the well-documented limitations of existing protection capacity in a broad range of countries (not only Greece and Turkey) suggest the next crisis for the European Union will not be far behind.

Through the deal, leaders hope to send a message to smugglers and would-be asylum seekers beyond EU borders. But they will also send a message to other host countries—including Turkey—that providing protection to large populations is a fungible task: should governments face the prospect of domestic unpopularity, the obligation to protect becomes secondary. This, for overstretched countries such as Lebanon, is an important memo, and may bolster efforts in major host countries to make conditions untenable for their existing refugee populations, leaving refugees with fewer and fewer alternatives. In focusing upon the most visible perceived threat, the problem has once again been squeezed elsewhere rather than resolved.

Hungary Violates Human Rights in Its Treatment of Refugees

Amnesty International

In the following viewpoint, Amnesty International accuses the nation of Hungary of violating international law in its handling of refugees. Amnesty International, a human rights organization, says that Hungary is violating human rights through policies designed to protect the country at the expense of those seeking asylum. Representatives of the group call on the European Union to denounce the Hungarian treatment of refugees.

As you read, consider the following questions:

1. Has Hungary spent more money on assisting refugees or on keeping them out of the country?
2. What tools does Hungary used to prevent refugees from seeking asylum?
3. Where are refugees and asylum seekers housed when they arrive in Budapest, the capital of Hungary?

The Hungarian government has invested more than 100 million euros on razor-wire fencing and border controls to keep refugees and migrants out, triple the amount it spends yearly on receiving asylum seekers, Amnesty International revealed in a new briefing published today.

"Hungary: EU must formally warn Hungary over refugee crisis violations," Amnesty International, October 8, 2015. Reprinted by permission.

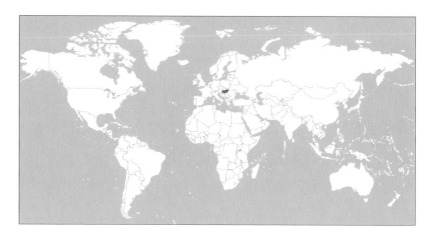

The briefing, Fenced Out, outlines how Hungary's draconian measures to control its borders have repeatedly violated international law. As EU ministers gather in Luxembourg today for high-level meetings to discuss the crisis, Amnesty International is calling on the EU to hold Hungary to account for its human rights failures and to protect people on the move by creating safer, legal routes before winter hits.

"Hungary is a few razor-wire coils away from completely sealing off its borders with Croatia and Serbia. Even those that do manage to squeeze through the key-hole are almost certain to be returned to Balkan countries of transit," said John Dalhusien, Amnesty International Director for Europe and Central Asia.

"Hungary is effectively transforming itself into a refugee protection free zone, with blatant disregard for its human rights obligations and the obvious need to work with other EU and Balkan countries to find collective, humane solutions to the current crisis," said John Dalhuisen.

The combination of building razor-wire fences and criminalizing those who do break through and enter the country irregularly, as well as the rush to return them to Balkan transit countries, is designed to isolate Hungary from the global and European refugee crisis. This comes at the wholesale expense of the respect for human rights.

Amnesty International is calling on the EU member States and institutions to prevent further escalation of human rights violations in Hungary by activating the preventive mechanism foreseen under Article 7(1) of the Treaty of the European Union. The mechanism allows the European Council to issue a warning to member states where there is "a clear risk of a serious breach" of the respect for the rule of law and human rights.

"The EU has the power to trigger formal discussions with Hungary over its appalling treatment of refugees and migrants and send a clear message that 'enough is enough' to those States that disregard EU and international law. The EU should do this before it is too late," said Iverna McGowan, Acting Director of Amnesty International's European Institutions Office.

"Scrutiny of the human rights situation in Hungary has repeatedly fallen through the cracks, with member states and institutions endlessly passing the buck on who is ultimately responsible for upholding human rights in the EU. This gap must be urgently bridged with a stronger response to human rights violations by EU member States and institutions alike."

Amnesty International drew on testimony and observations compiled from extensive in-country research in September. Researchers examined the police treatment of refugees and migrants, reception conditions, as well as the application of new restrictions on access to asylum in the country.

The Hungarian Parliament has been ushering in new laws resulting in an aggressive response that includes flanking its borders with soldiers and police authorized to use rubber bullets, tear gas grenades and pyrotechnical devices. Armoured vehicles mounted with machine guns, and soldiers armed with Special Forces style firearms have been positioned along the border with Croatia.

Testimonies reveal the repeated use of excessive force by the Hungarian authorities.

Hiba, a 32-year-old asylum-seeker from Iraq, suffered a fracture to her thigh after being pushed by a Hungarian police officer against a wall at a train station in Budapest.

"I have been living in uncertainty and stress for months," said Hiba, now in Germany. "We are now waiting for a decision on our asylum claim but people [other asylum-seekers] are telling us we might be rejected and sent back to Hungary and then back to Iraq. But there is no way how we can go back to Tikrit, it's not safe."

Other new laws have allowed Hungary to place Serbia on a list of safe countries of origin and transit, to which the asylum seekers are now to be returned, without regard for the severe obstacles they face in accessing protection in that country. Refugees and asylum-seekers who enter irregularly also face criminal prosecution, in breach of international human rights law.

The briefing details the Hungarian authorities' pitiful humanitarian response with a complete lack of adequate reception facilities. In the absence of essential supplies such as food and tents, refugees and asylum seekers massed at Budapest's main train stations, Keleti, Nyugati and Deli, had to rely on support provided largely by volunteers and through donations.

"I want to start a new life in peace... They are treating us like animals, worse than animals," said Dina, a 46-year-old Syrian woman who had been taken into police custody and kept for 16 hours without food or water. "It prevents us to stay here. We feel that we are not welcome."

The briefing highlights the massive disparity between the bulk of anti-immigration spending compared to the budget for processing asylum seekers' applications. Some 98 million euros have been funneled into the Hungary-Serbia border fence, at least three times the 27.5 million euros budget of the Office of Immigration and Nationality for 2015.

"The cost of these abhorrent anti-refugee operations is staggering and comes at the price of the rights, health and well-being of thousands of people," said John Dalhuisen.

"This money would be far more wisely invested in saving lives and improving futures. It's time for all EU member states to urgently invest in a compassionate and coordinated solution."

Get Rid of Refugee Camps

Kristy Siegfried

In the following viewpoint, Kristy Siegfried criticizes refugee camps. She suggests that confining refugees to camps should be a last resort, as the camps limit the rights and freedoms of refugees. Allowing refugees to live and work among local citizens improves their lives and allows them to contribute to the economy. Getting rid of all refugee camps will not be easy, however. It will require convincing host countries of the benefits of integrating refugees, and training refugees to enter the job market. Kristy Siegfried is a journalist and editor covering migration and refugee issues for IRIN, an independent media group.

As you read, consider the following questions:

1. What percentage of the world's refugees live in refugee camps?
2. Why do many host countries prefer keeping refugees in camps rather than integrating them into cities?
3. Are refugees who are allowed to work usually able to support themselves?

For years, the images most commonly associated with refugees have been of sprawling, dusty camps populated by rows of tents sheltering thousands of men, women and children with little to occupy them besides queuing for aid handouts.

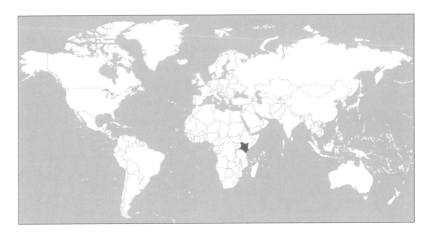

The reality is that only just over one third of the world's 17 million refugees live in camps today. The rest choose to live in cities or communities where a more independent, if precarious, existence is possible.

The international humanitarian community has been slow to respond to this reality, but is now scrambling to catch up, especially in view of the crisis in Syria which has so far produced over three million refugees, the majority of whom are living in cities in neighbouring countries.

The UN Refugee Agency (UNHCR), in particular, has struggled to adapt its traditionally camp-based model to fulfil its mandate of ensuring that all refugees have access to protection and assistance, wherever they may live.

In 2009, it released a policy statement on refugee protection and solutions in urban areas which recognized urban areas as "a legitimate place for refugees to enjoy their rights".

Now it has gone a significant step further with the release of an "Alternatives to Camps" policy which commits the agency to actively pursue alternatives to camps whenever possible. It is the first official recognition by UNHCR that camps should be a last resort rather than the default response to refugee influxes, and has been widely welcomed by the refugee rights community as representing a major, if overdue, shift in the agency's approach.

Between the UNHCR's establishment in the early 1950s and the installation of its current High Commissioner Antonio Guterres in 2005, "there was a widespread assumption within the humanitarian community that refugees belonged in camps," according to Jeff Crisp, formerly the agency's head of policy and evaluation, writing in a blog for advocacy group Refugees International, where he now serves as senior director for policy and advocacy.

Camps becoming harder to fund

Keeping refugees in camps has not only been logistically far more convenient for aid providers, but has often been the preference of host states who view camps as minimizing both the perceived security threat posed by refugees and their burden on local communities and economies. However, as refugee crises have become more protracted, with over six million refugees now living in exile for five or more years, camps have become increasingly difficult to fund.

"A lot of funding goes to new emergencies but within as little as 18 months, if the emergency is not continuing, there's a falling away of donor support," said Steven Corliss, director of UNHCR's programme management and support division. As support diminishes programmes such as secondary education are the first casualties, but eventually even basic services come under pressure. Recently, the World Food Programme had to cut food rations for a third of all African refugees, the majority of them long-term refugees confined to camps.

UNHCR's new policy acknowledges that camps remain a necessary feature of the humanitarian landscape, particularly in the context of emergencies and where host governments insist on them, but adds that "they nevertheless represent a compromise that limits the rights and freedoms of refugees and too often remain after the emergency phase and the essential reasons for their existence have passed."

"Camps should be the exception and, to the extent possible, a temporary measure," states the policy.

Corliss of UNHCR explained that the policy was the result of an internal discussion and "a conviction that this is the right and most humane approach…

"The idea is to give people a meaningful choice and the opportunity to live a more dignified life," he told IRIN.

Sonia Ben Ali, founding director of Urban Refugees, an NGO, described the new policy as "a milestone" and welcomed its rights-based approach. "It plays a very strong role in showing how UNHCR recognizes that camps are not the proper conditions for refugees to live in," she told IRIN.

Getting host states on board could be tricky

She added that the success of the policy would depend to a large extent on how effective advocacy efforts will be, particularly in convincing host governments that alternatives to camps are not only better for refugees, but can also produce better outcomes for local economies and host communities.

"We need to address the [security and economic] concerns of host states, and for this we really need an evidence base," she said.

Corliss agreed that there was a need to gather more evidence that alternatives to the camps' approaches could benefit host communities, for example by allowing aid agencies to invest more in local infrastructure instead of funding parallel service delivery systems in camps.

"Refugees come with assets; they have a lot of human potential that can help stimulate the economy. It's very important to document that so we can advocate for it."

Researchers from Oxford University's Humanitarian Innovation Project have begun this task with a recent study from Uganda showing that the majority of refugees who gained permission to live and work outside designated refugee settlements, found ways to sustain themselves without aid.

However, not everyone is confident that even evidence-based advocacy efforts will be enough to overcome resistance from host states that often has less to do with real concerns about refugees over-burdening local communities than with what Lucy Hovil, a senior researcher at the International Refugee Rights Initiative, referred to in a recent article as "realpolitik".

In Kenya, for example, the dominant narrative that Somali refugees represent a security threat, has seen thousands of Somalis living in Nairobi pushed back to camps in the past six months.

Michael Kagan, co-director of the Immigration Clinic at Nevada University's William S. Boyd School of Law, described the alternatives to camps' policy as encouraging but "still aspirational".

"The missing link is to explain how host governments can be persuaded to let refugees have more autonomy," he said. "What is still not clear is how UNHCR will react when host governments refuse to abandon camps. Will UNHCR cooperate? Will they refuse? How hard will UNHCR push? Will UNHCR fall back on platitudes rather than standards? This, we don't know."

Change needed in livelihoods support

Corliss of UNHCR acknowledged that "creating an enabling environment in terms of law and policy" would be essential to the new policy's success, but also pointed to the need for a "fundamental transformation in the way we do livelihoods programming". Whereas in the past, livelihoods support has been used "as a kind of occupational therapy, to keep people busy in camps", Corliss said UNHCR was moving towards "a much more hard-headed, market-oriented approach" that would help refugees acquire the appropriate skills to enter a host country's job market or to start a small business.

Corliss added that bringing refugees to the point where they can achieve sustainable livelihoods requires "comprehensive support over a period of time".

In recent years, UNHCR and other aid agencies have been experimenting with various ways of delivering that support to refugees dispersed throughout urban areas. "Cash-based interventions will be very important," said Corliss, and have the added benefit of stimulating local economies. UNHCR is already making use of cash-based interventions in 94 operations around the world. In the longer term, however, there will be a need to work with development partners to strengthen local infrastructure such as public health systems.

"This is a policy that's extremely ambitious and is going to have to be progressively implemented," he told IRIN.

Guidance to help field staff operationalize the policy is still being developed and UNHCR will need buy-in from partners, including international NGOs, other UN agencies and donors, but most importantly host governments.

Kagan pointed out that outside camps, what refugees needed even more than aid was rights - "the right to work, the right to send your kids to school. These are the things refugees need in cities," said Kagan. "They have to have rights to be able to rebuild their lives in dignity. And that requires government buy-in."

Aid Organizations Waste Money

DMG Media

The following viewpoint examines how aid money targeted for refugee support is spent. The article claims that money is often wasted at refugee camps. Improvements that would save money in the long run are declined and funds are instead funneled to bureaucrats and contractors. Aid workers are accused of competing against each other for resources and lying about their successes. DMG Media is a national newspaper and website publisher in the UK.

As you read, consider the following questions:

1. What percentage of wealth in the United Kingdom goes to aid to refugees?
2. How is bureaucracy leading to ineffective financial choices for refugee camps?
3. According to the article, why was water trucked in and out of Zaatari (a refugee camp in Jordan)?

Shocking multi-million-pound waste and paralysing bureaucracy at the United Nations have been exposed by a former senior official from the organisation – which receives vast sums from the British taxpayer each year.

Killian Kleinschmidt was the manager of a sprawling camp for Syrian refugees in Zaatari, Jordan.

"UN refugee camp chief: We wasted millions. Why? Because—reveals whistleblower in a stunning admission—we were obsessed by photos of stars in our T-shirts," DMG Media, April 18, 2016. Reprinted by permission.

A veteran of 25 years with the UN High Commissioner for Refugees (UNHCR), the Austrian aid expert has revealed how the organisation was dogged by infighting and an obsession with celebrities.

And he has exposed how senior aid bureaucrats lied about caring for thousands more children than they actually did.

His concerns will again raise serious doubts about why the UK is spending 0.7 per cent of its wealth – £12 billion last year – on aid, funding many questionable projects and unaccountable multi-national organisations.

The Zaatari camp houses about 79,580 displaced Syrians and costs about £320,000 a day to run.

Prince Charles and actor Michael Sheen have both visited the camp, which no one doubts is providing vital humanitarian care.

However, Mr Kleinschmidt highlighted how bureaucracy has led to colossal waste in energy costs for what is in effect a small city, after UNHCR passed up the opportunity to install money-saving solar panels.

After an initial outlay, the panels would have helped the camp avoid energy bills of about £700,000 a month, but bureaucratic resistance meant the opportunity was missed.

Mr Kleinschmidt said: 'A company from the US came in early 2014 and said it would cost $ 20 million.

'They offered help with the engineering, and said they would donate $5 million, leaving us to find $15 million for solar panels and to manage production of power.'

Although the UNHCR said no, the German government has now agreed to pay for the solar panels, but the camp will have to wait until 2017 for them to be installed.

If the panels had been installed in 2014, it would have saved nearly £25 million in energy costs – much more than the initial set-up fees.

Another project, on sanitation, showed how the UN was needlessly wasting money on contractors.

Mr Kleinschmidt said: 'In Zaatari, Unicef [the UN's Children's Emergency Fund] spent $30 million on water and sanitation – clean water coming in and dirty water and garbage going out.

'It would have been much cheaper to have set up a piped water system, but they were bringing it in by truck and are still trucking it in there to a large extent because that ensures the money keeps coming to fund all the bureaucrats involved. From Unicef it goes down to the next international NGO [Non-Governmental Organisation] and then down the line to the Jordanian contractor who owns the trucks, and before a single drop of water has been delivered, you've spent $15 million out of the $30 million.'

Mr Kleinschmidt, who ran the camp from 2013 and left the UN in late 2014, was also shocked by the outright lies of aid colleagues.

He said: 'I remember in 2013, Unicef were making a big story about how 15,000 kids go to school at the camp, but it wasn't true, it was a lie. You might have that many enrolled, but only 3,000 to 4,000 were going into the school. How can you put something out which is simply not true?

'They were very angry with me because I spoiled their story.'

He added: 'Zaatari confirmed to me that the [aid] chain makes no sense.

'In a world of maybe only $23 billion of humanitarian aid, one has to be a bit more careful how it's spent and more innovative in our partnerships.'

Mr Kleinschmidt, who after becoming disillusioned with the UN started his own aid consultancy, said that vicious infighting between the organisation's departments made aid work ineffective. 'The key issue is competition for resources between different agencies. The UN shouldn't worry about which agency has the nicest T-shirts and the nicest caps, or which celebrity is your ambassador.

'We're supposed to work all together so that agencies with different skills are all pulling in one direction but of course that doesn't happen.

'Getting away from all that pointless competition would help tremendously.'

Britain gave the UN £518 million in 2014, the last year for which figures are available, and a total of £2.1 billion for the five years starting from 2010.

Mr Kleinschmidt said that, after his long career delivering aid, he had concluded: 'Looking at people only as victims and recipients of charity has to change as well.

'The way the system works is pushing people to dependency. You either become very cynical and negative or you try to change it.

'I've seen most of the system at work – I'm one of those guys you might describe as a 'frustrated senior aid official'.

The UNHCR did not respond to our requests for a comment by last night.

Periodical and Internet Sources Bibliography

The following articles have been selected to supplement the diverse views presented in this chapter.

Charlotte Alfred, "Expert Discussion: The Future of the E.U.-Turkey Refugee Deal", News Deeply, August 30, 2016. https://www.newsdeeply.com/refugees/articles/2016/08/30/expert-discussion-the-future-of-the-e-u-turkey-refugee-deal

Bill Chappell, "7 Targeted Countries React To Trump's Ban On Immigration," NPR, January 30, 2017. http://www.npr.org/sections/thetwo-way/2017/01/30/512438879/7-targeted-countries-react-to-trumps-ban-on-immigration

"EU-Turkey Agreement Failing Refugee Women and Girls", Women's Refugee Commission, August 2016. https://www.womensrefugeecommission.org/images/zdocs/EU-Turkey-Refugee-Agreement-Failing.pdf

Ashley Kirk, "Refugee crisis: How do European countries' attitudes differ on refugees?" The Telegraph, September 16, 2015. http://www.telegraph.co.uk/news/uknews/immigration/11863452/Refugee-crisis-How-do-European-countries-attitudes-differ-on-refugees.html

"Migrant crisis: A Syrian's struggle to become German", BBC, October 16, 2016. http://www.bbc.com/news/world-europe-37647852

"Migrant crisis: EU-Turkey deal is 'working'", BBC, April 24, 2016. http://www.bbc.com/news/world-europe-36121083

Muna Mire, "8 Women Respond to Trump's Immigration Ban", Elle, February 2, 2017. http://www.elle.com/culture/career-politics/news/a42640/muslim-women-respond-to-trump-immigration-ban/

Erica Rawles, "Refugee Camps: Temporary Solutions to Long-Term Problems", The Borgen Project, August 10, 2016. https://borgenproject.org/refugee-camps-temporary-solutions/

"Refugee crisis: How different countries have responded", BBC, September 1, 2015. http://www.bbc.co.uk/newsbeat/article/34114936/refugee-crisis-how-different-countries-have-responded

Jennifer Williams, "From "shameful" to "well done": world leaders speak out on Trump's immigrant ban," Vox, January 29, 2017.

http://www.vox.com/world/2017/1/29/14427074/world-leaders-reactions-trump-refugee-immigration-ban

USA TODAY College staff, "How universities are responding to Trump's travel ban", USA TODAY, January 29, 2017. http://college.usatoday.com/2017/01/29/how-universities-are-responding-to-trumps-travel-ban/

GLOBALVIEWPOINTS

CHAPTER 5

Better Solutions for Addressing Migrant and Refugee Crises

Every Country Needs Unique Solutions

International Labour Organization

In chapter 3, viewpoint 3, a report from the International Labour Organization explored how the Syrian refugee crisis is affecting neighboring countries. In the following viewpoint, another excerpt from the same report offers more specific and detailed solutions for two of the affected countries, Lebanon and Egypt. The different challenges and recommended solutions show the complexity of the issue and suggest that no single answer will work in every country.

As you read, consider the following questions:

1. In Lebanon, who is especially affected by the increase in unemployment and informal employment? (Informal employment is the part of the economy not taxed or monitored by the government.)
2. When does the plan for Lebanon recommend that human labor is used instead of machinery?
3. Why is Egypt's plan for development of the food sector not limited to refugees?

Programme Outline: Lebanon

In December 2015 it was estimated that 1,069,111 Syrian refugees live in Lebanon, which is more than a quarter of Lebanon's estimated 4.3 million native residents.[10] The sheer scale of the

"The ILO Response To The Syrian Refugee Crisis," International Labour Organization, February 2016. Reprinted by permission ©2016, ILO.

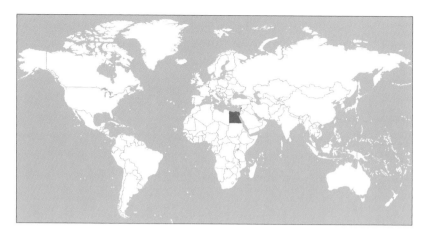

influx vis- à-vis Lebanon's population has severely affected the country's socioeconomic situation. The crisis has also resulted in unprecedented restrictions on Syrians entering Lebanon in late 2014. Pre-existing labour market challenges have been exacerbated by the crisis, doubling the number of unemployed in Lebanon, and increasing the informality rate of the country by 10 per cent.[11] Young Lebanese women and men are disproportionally affected by the refugee crisis.[12] A large proportion of young people who work do so informally and in insecure working conditions.[13] The overall unemployment rate is estimated to be at 12 per cent.[14]

While poverty in Lebanon has, so far, been primarily concentrated in small pockets in suburbs of large towns, poverty in rural areas has remained particularly acute, [15] where Syrian refugees now reside. At present, Syrian refugees have to sign a 'pledge not to work' when renewing their residency status, making any kind of income generation activity illegal for them. 70 per cent of displaced Syrians now live below the poverty line, an increase of 20 percentage points in one year, and 50 per cent do not have the income needed to afford the "Survival Minimum Expenditure Basket" (SMEB). This is particularly severe in the Bekaa, Akkar and Tripoli areas where these proportions are at 70-80 per cent.[16] Those Syrian refugees who work do so in low skilled activities, primarily in services (36 per cent) and the traditional sectors using Syrian labour, i.e. agriculture (28 per cent) and construction (12 per cent).[17] Syrian refugees rely, almost exclusively, on temporary and informal work, with a monthly income of less than USD 300, on average.[18]

The ILO response

In order to provide an appropriate response to the Syrian refugee crisis in the Lebanese context, the ILO Regional Office for the Arab States implements a strategy, as a partner, under the Lebanon Crisis Response Plan 2015-16. [19] This builds on existing programmes in Lebanon through three inter-related components:

1. Assessing the impact of the Syrian refugee crisis in Lebanon on decent work
2. Enhancing access to employment opportunities and livelihoods in host communities
3. Combating the worst forms of child labour and unacceptable forms of work

At present, the ILO contributes to realizing the objectives of the Lebanon Crisis Response Plan 2015-16 through three interlinked programmes, as described below.

Supporting evidence-based policy development to ensure an employment-rich national response embedded in the principles of decent work

Project: Enhancing the capacity of the Ministry of Labour to develop strategies for labour market policies, data collection, and analysis Overall objective Ministry of Labour and National Employment Office have enhanced institutional and technical capacity to develop strategies for labour market policies, data collection, and analysis.

Brief Description In order to cope with the adverse economic effects of the crisis, the Government of Lebanon has initiated policy reforms to spur job creation, particularly in refugee host communities. In support of this policy, the ILO has initiated three complementary projects:

1. Strengthening labour administration and inspection: based on a technical needs assessment of the Labour Administration Office of Lebanon's Ministry of Labour, several recommendations have been made to ensure good governance of labour-related matters and national systems of labour administration with the aim of social and economic development. Future ILO measures will focus on the implementation of priority recommendations for the effective delivery of services by the MOL within the context of the Syrian refugee crisis.

2. Reforming the National Employment Office: The ILO has conducted a legal review and helped draft a decree to restructure the National Employment Office and refine its mandate to collect labour market statistics, contribute to labour market analysis, and monitor and coordinate the operations of private employment services in Lebanon.

3. Implementing a labour force and living conditions survey: The ILO and the Central

Administration for Statistics (CAS), Lebanon's official statistics body, have launched a project entitled the "Labour Force and Households Living Conditions Survey" (LFHLCS). The survey will be the first to produce estimates at the national, governorate, and district levels to highlight regional disparities and characteristics. Such indicators will inform policy-making and the labour market information systems that are instrumental to human development planning aiming to address the effects of the Syrian refugee crisis on the Lebanese labour market.

Enhancing access to employment opportunities and livelihoods for crisis-affected communities

Project: Agricultural Livelihoods, Employment and Income for Vulnerable People in Rural Lebanon affected by the Syrian Conflict Overall objective Improved productive employment and decent work opportunities through the promotion of sustainable enterprises and by strengthening the employability of vulnerable groups.

Brief Description The project aims to promote the employment and livelihoods of vulnerable groups affected by the Syria crisis through two distinct but interlinked components: enhancing the employability of youth in agriculture and improving agricultural income and employment through value chain development embedded in an inclusive LED approach. Firstly, it will expand on its existing collaboration with the Ministry of Agriculture in enhancing and strengthening the agricultural vocational training programme provided by the ministry through collaboration with the private sector in order to increase the employability of the youth. This will be carried out by converting the current Baccalaureate Technique into a Dual System, a system that integrates learning outcomes to be attained through apprenticeships. The second component consists of an expansion of a current ILO project which aims at enhancing the resilience of entrepreneurs including farmers and workers affected by the Syria crisis in Lebanon in rural areas focusing on Akkar – an area that has the highest poverty incidence and hosts very high numbers of refugees. The project interventions are based on the results and recommendations of the value chains analysis of two agriculture sub-sectors (potato and leafy greens) in 2014/2015. It strengthens the effectiveness of key market actors and institutions in addressing and improving market underperformance, developing and sustaining local economic opportunities along the value chains, as well as reducing decent work gap in the two value chains.

Project: Creating decent work opportunities for Syrian refugees and host communities in Lebanon through infrastructure improvement: a win-win approach

Overall objective

1) Jobs for Lebanese unemployed as well as legal work opportunities for a minimum of 25,000 Syrian refugees created, leading to immediate and long-term economic development gains;

and 2) the Ministry of Labour has a strengthened role in improving the functioning of the Lebanese labour market.

Brief Description

Legal work opportunities for 25,000 Syrian refugees will be achieved in three ways:

1. Moving towards formalizing unskilled and semi-skilled jobs currently illegally done by Syrian refugees by engaging with employers and contractor organizations, ensuring application of national labour standards and inclusion of decent work principles.

2. Developing work opportunities for Syrian refugees and Lebanese job seekers through the implementation of infrastructure projects using the Employment intensive investment Programme (EIIP) approach. The components included are:

   a. Agricultural Feeder Roads: This initiative aims to develop periodic maintenance for Lebanon's network of rural roads, which will improve their condition and create longterm jobs.

   b. Water Catchment: In order to address the lack of a standardized water management system, this initiative aims to build water catchment systems for small farms in Lebanon. c. Terracing and Land Reclamation: This initiative aims to carry out terracing in order to create arable land, protect slopes and counter erosion.

3. Engaging in policy level dialogue with the Ministry of Labour and National Contractors Associations to formalize Decent Work Principles in the recruitment and contracting of labour for Lebanese and foreign workers including refugees.

Labour shall only be used in those cases where it is cost effective versus machinery, or where donor, contractor and government agree that, from a humanitarian perspective, labour shall be used to

16 provide income. The project will be implemented in partnership with stake holders including the Ministries of Labour, Public Work and Agriculture. An emphasis will be placed on building the capacities of local partners. A specialised team will oversee and advice project management on social issues, including gender balancing and worker protection. Institutional Experts will build the capacity of the Ministry of Labour to conduct labour inspection, skills forecasting and formulating a Labour Market Strategy.

Combating the increasing incidence of child labour

Project: Reducing Child Labour in Lebanon

Overall objective To contribute to the elimination of child labour, especially its worst forms, among Syrian refugees and host communities in Lebanon.

Brief Description The project will endeavour to provide a robust response to child labour on the ground, targeting Syrian, Lebanese as well as other children. Its objectives are the following:

1. 500 Children in target areas withdrawn or prevented from involvement in child labour, through the strengthening and upgrading of two child support centres, enabling them to provide a comprehensive package of services to children involved in or at risk of child labour.

2. Capacity of duty bearers and stakeholders built in addressing child labour. This objective will be reached through the training of 1,200 teachers and school counsellors as well as 150 social workers on preventing and addressing Child Labour, as well as the rolling of the 'Guidelines to Prevent School Drop Outs and Child Labour'. Activities to address child labour will be integrated in the activities of municipal authorities with 150 Municipal officials trained. [70] Inspectors and employer representatives will be trained on the 'Indicators of Hazardous Labour' (manual). Essential equipment to enhance the capacity of key stakeholders will be provided.

3. Awareness on child labour raised with a focus on change in behaviour and attitude, through a Knowledge, Attitude and Practices (KAP) survey on Child Labour to identify gaps and the development of a child labour awareness strategy.

4. Child/youth volunteers attached to local authorities, Community-Based Organisations and NGOs trained and mobilized to address child labour.

[...]

Programme Outline: Egypt

Despite the absence of a common border with Syria, Egypt has admitted a high number of Syrian refugees. In September 2015, it was estimated that the number of officially registered Syrian refugees in Egypt reached 128,000 women, men and children and that an equal number of Syrians live unregistered in the country. Although the number of Syrian refugees in Egypt is relatively small compared with countries bordering Syria, the concentration of refugees in certain governorates (Giza, Greater Cairo, Alexandria and Qalyubia) has placed additional pressure on the delivery of basic services and calls for targeted assistance in relation to food, health, education, livelihoods and basic needs.

The ILO response

An area-based approach is foreseen to support both Syrian refugees and local residents in the Egyptian communities affected so as to improve basic delivery systems, income-generating activities and social cohesion. The means in which this will be done are described below.

Food sector promotion for urban refugees: Value chain development in Greater Cairo's food services sector

Recognizing the need to understand the employment and economic potential of Syrian refugees in Egypt, and as part of an overall cooperation agreement between the ILO and UNHCR, a project to assess the economic sectors and subsectors of high employment potential for Syrians in Egypt was implemented by the ILO in the period 1 December 2013—31 March 2014. This project used a participatory and gender-sensitive value chain analysis approach, the results of which were disseminated and shared with all stakeholders through a national workshop. The study showed that the food sector absorbs large numbers of Syrians and has potential for economic value addition for both Egyptian nationals and Syrians. Based on the results of this analysis, the ILO has developed a project proposal to strengthen and upgrade the food sector value chain in the most vulnerable and impacted communities. This will entail:

1. Setting up an information database providing information on suppliers, business tools and services, standards, local policies, and other relevant market information

2. Establishing a call centre to facilitate home delivery

3. Organizing a training programme with a specific focus on marketing in Egypt's food sector. It is foreseen that these activities will help build a stronger business development services market that responds to the most pressing needs in terms of services to the target groups

4. A start-up programme for small restaurants and food stands that selects participants with potential and adapts a start-up training package for this target audience [21]

These activities will lead to more and better jobs and livelihoods for both Syrian refugees and Egyptians working in the food sector. The project aims to reach at least 5,000 market actors, of whom at least 50 per cent are refugees. By not focusing exclusively on Syrians, the project aims to show that the interventions are contributing to the overall growth of the food services sector in major urban centres in Egypt with shared benefits. As the UNHCR and the ILO plan to engage in more pilot projects in other regions, lessons learned from this project will inform the planning and development of interventions in similar projects as well.

Improving and sustaining basic needs of the most vulnerable men, women, children and youth

In addition, the ILO has been actively engaged with other UN organizations in the design of Egypt's country response to reduce vulnerability and improve livelihoods for Egyptians and Syrians in host communities. This also falls under the 3RP umbrella and overall aims are as follows:

1. Building the capacity of national and local partners to improve the delivery systems for social protection

2. Promoting job creation through enterprise development

3. Improving matchmaking activities to facilitate young people's transition to work

These Solutions Will Fix the Refugee Crisis in Europe

Giles Merritt and Shada Islam

In the following excerpted viewpoint, Giles Merritt and Shada Islam state that most ideas for dealing with Europe's refugee crisis are based on flawed assumptions. They claim that the Muslim refugees can and should be integrated. They also argue that the European Union needs to do more to aid economic development in Africa, in order to prevent future waves of immigrants searching for a better life in Europe. The authors list 10 ideas that they feel will better address the problems. Giles Merritt and Shada Islam are part of Friends of Europe, is a think tank focused on creating positive change in Europe.

As you read, consider the following questions:

1. How could the exploding population in African countries affect Europe in the future?
2. Why are young workers necessary to every country?
3. How many Muslims currently live in Europe?

The plethora of ideas for dealing with Europe's refugee and economic migrant crisis centre chiefly on two assumptions: that tougher measures can staunch the flow, and that the flow is temporary. Both are wrong. A third assumption exacerbating the political difficulties within the EU is that it will be impossible to integrate the newcomers because they are mostly Muslim. It will

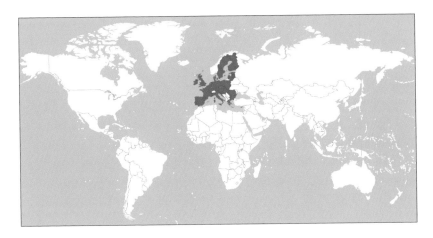

not be easy, but it's far from impossible. Recent terrorist attacks in Brussels, Paris, Ankara and elsewhere have of course further complicated matters.

Policymakers across the EU have so far been doing almost everything wrong. And far from safeguarding the delicate political equilibrium between EU countries achieved over six decades, it has become the first casualty.

The seriousness of the challenges confronting EU countries is beyond doubt. The speed and scale of the influx of people is placing intolerable strains on limited housing and administrative resources. Temporary or transitional arrangements have been rushed into place in the six of the EU's 28 countries that have so far borne the brunt of the crisis. The still greater challenge will be the more permanent adjustments Europe must make, and it is these that this Discussion Paper addresses.

Europe has a mixed and not very encouraging record on integrating immigrants, both socially and economically. This dates chiefly from when the volume of arrivals was more manageable. Lessons must be drawn from those shortcomings. At the same time, EU national and local authorities must grapple with very immediate problems of relocating, housing, employing and in some cases educating newcomers. EU-level responses have to date been focused far more on burden-sharing than on how to resolve these integration challenges.

On top of this, there is the 'security' dimension of the crisis. The increasingly fierce anti-Muslim diatribes of some Eastern European leaders are exacerbating the existing anti-Islam mood in other parts of Europe, making discussion of integration so difficult as to be virtually impossible. The deafening silence of most mainstream politicians contrasts with the strident voices of Far-Right populists. German Chancellor Angela Merkel remains the exception.

An equally significant facet of the debate is the absence of longer-term thinking. The spotlight is on migratory pressures in Middle Eastern and North African countries, and this is eclipsing the greater problem for years ahead of the population explosion in most of Africa's 54 nation states. The EU's efforts to aid economic development in those countries need a substantial boost.

The African continent's present population of some 1.2 billion will by mid-century have more or less doubled, placing enormous strains on employment and housing. The drift to Africa's cities is expected to boost the proportion of city-dwellers from one-third to two-thirds, severely exacerbating living conditions unless accompanied by a dramatic acceleration in economic development. The emigration of tens of millions of Africans in search of a better life risks dwarfing the crisis now confronting Europe.

The exodus northwards of people fleeing war-torn Syria, Afghanistan and Iraq is, meanwhile, creating a chaotic and politically-explosive muddle. Europe's response has been messy and chaotic. Decisions taken in Brussels are not followed up. The preferred solution has been to erect unworkable barriers that run counter to international conventions and Europe's own much-vaunted 'values' and anyway are doomed to fail.

Yet there's no shortage of good ideas for turning the refugee and economic migrant crisis to Europe's advantage. Here are ten suggestions that could transform this politically-toxic crisis into a win-win proposition. All either run counter to existing practices and policies within the EU, or are not covered by them.

This Discussion Paper sets out to raise issues and policy directions that require attention. It also launches Migration Action, Friends of Europe's new initiative for involving a wider range of specialists whose expertise can complement the efforts of EU actors and others as they confront the new migratory challenges.

1. The European Council Should Acknowledge the Benefits of Immigration

Much of the conventional wisdom that has shaped European responses to the migrant and refugee crisis has been wrong-headed. Opinion formers must challenge the widely-held idea that there' s only a finite pool of jobs, so that newcomers threaten job-holders. The European public must be encouraged to understand that newcomers also bring fresh demand and so spur growth, and that would be given a strong push by EU leaders' reference in a European Council to the expected shrinkage of Europe's labour force in the years ahead.

The media, as primary shapers of public opinion, have a vital role to play in alerting people across Europe that a failure to embrace immigration carries heavy costs, especially for their children and their children's children. By mid-century, the ratio between working-age people making up the active population and those who are retired and drawing a pension will have shrunk dramatically from 4:1 today to just 2:1. The only way to fund social security systems will be to import young people as workers and taxpayers. That was the 2010 message of a 'Wise Men's' group led by former Spanish premier Felipe Gonzalez when it warned that Europe needs 100m immigrants over the 40 years to 2050.

The rise of populist parties in many EU countries has done nothing to encourage mainstream politicians, including mayors and local leaders, to be more courageous on immigration. Yet the shrinkage of ageing Europe' s workforce, and in many cases national populations, is eye-catching. Until the refugee crisis broke in 2015 Germany's population of 82 million was expected by 2030 to have shrunk by 6 million, and by 2060 to just 65 million.

Some recent forecasts instead see a possible stabilisation of the overall population, although the ageing factor remains a major problem. For Europe as a whole, the next 20 years could well see a faster dwindling of the working age population than at any time since the Black Death in the mid-14th century.

Economies, most experts agree, grow fastest when the active labour force is growing. And that means capitalising on the current surge of immigration and capitalising on the fact that last year a third of the newcomers arriving in Sweden from Syria had a university degree, and when some German observers were reporting that 70% of Syrian refugees there had a 'middle class background'.

2. Civil Society Must Craft a Positive New Conversation of Integration

The challenges are not only economic but also cultural. Europe's task will be to integrate millions of Muslim newcomers into historically Christian societies at a time when the fanaticism of Islamic militants is plunging the Arab world into turmoil and threatening Europeans' security. Despite the anti-Islam vitriol and the focus on terrorism, millions of European Muslims live in peace as tax-paying citizens. And although the over-arching narrative presents Muslims as deeply religious, some studies suggest that relatively few Muslims in Europe belong to religious organisations, including mosques.

Europe therefore needs a new narrative on integration - especially of Muslims - and it needs it urgently. Such an exercise will require determination and vision, good arguments backed by facts, and much better communication.

Integration requires a ' whole of society' approach. Canada's large-scale and ambitious immigration strategy has demonstrated that tools ranging from sports clubs to church and mosque-related activities have a powerful influence on the absorption of younger immigrants into the societies of host countries. The role of local authorities is especially important.

First, the facts. Despite the shrill headlines of a clash of cultures and conflicting values, Europe is home to about 44 million Muslims, of whom 19 million live in European Union countries. Muslims represent 8% of the population in France, 6% in Germany, 5% in Great Britain.

Far from fighting to change European societies, the majority of European Muslims are law-abiding citizens who pay their taxes and, according to the Open Society Institute, share the same concerns, needs and experiences as non-Muslims, including the quest for a 'better quality of education, improved housing, cleaner streets and [the tackling o anti-social behaviour and crime'.

The Institute adds that despite the populist rhetoric, an overwhelming majority of Muslims in France and Germany describe themselves as loyal to their country and see no contradiction between French/German and Muslim. Germany's Bertelsmann Foundation notes that Muslims in Germany 'feel closely connected' to the country and support the 'fundamental values' of German society. Muslims have become part of society, says the report, adding: 'There is no evidence supporting the common contention that Muslims are living in a separate, parallel society'.

The process of adaptation, accommodation and integration of Europe and Islam is well underway. Sons of Pakistani migrants to Britain include Sajid Javid, Britain's Secretary of State for Business, and Sadiq Khan, the new Mayor of London. At least 11 members of the European Parliament have a Muslim family background. Abdelkader Benali is a famous Dutch author of Moroccan descent. Zayn Malik headed one of Britain's most famous boy bands until he left the group recently.

Fashioning a new narrative on integration demands that Europe conducts a sensible conversation on refugees, migrants and Islam. People must move from talking about 'us' and 'them' to a more inclusive language of living in a shared space, with shared concerns and interests and, yes, even shared values. It also means tackling the concerns of people who feel anxious about the economic effects of immigration on themselves, their families, their jobs and their towns and cities. Although the public discourse on immigration has become poisonous, it is important to confront and talk about the pressure and benefits that immigration brings.

The discussion must be inclusive. Further polarisation between the anti-immigration groups and those favouring a more open Europe will not be helpful. The environment is more favourable to changing the narrative than many believe. The tragic terrorist attacks in Brussels and Paris and the focus on European 'foreign fighters' who have joined the so-called Islamic State in Syria has spotlighted the malaise and disaffection felt by many young Europeans of Muslim descent.

Muslims are becoming significantly more active in demanding equal rights as fully fledged citizens, organising themselves into pressure groups and emerging as influential politicians, entrepreneurs and cultural icons. However, this slow but steady recognition that all Europeans, whatever their religion, ethnic origins and cultural background, share a common space has not been translated into a rallying and attractive narrative.

Developing a new 'European immigration story' requires the joint efforts of politicians and policymakers, scholars as well as thought and religious leaders, civil society organisations, business representatives and the media. It means highlighting that Europe is a truly diverse continent which celebrates all its citizens, regardless of race and religion and recognises that if it is to compete on the global stage, it needs to capitalise on the talents of all its citizens.

The message should be clear: integration is a two-way street, requiring adjustment efforts by migrants and host societies. Newcomers must abide by existing rules so that they can become part of the conversation. But in exchange they should be accepted as fully fledged members of society.

Given the present sorry lack of representation of people of migrant background in national governments, parliaments and EU institutions, some form of 'affirmative action' or support for higher education, facilitation of job promotion is needed to encourage minorities to become active social participants. The EU institutions could make a start by doing this as regards their own recruitment policy. With European Parliament elections scheduled for 2019, the EU assembly should make sure that ethnic-minority politicians are included on their voting lists.

Closer monitoring of integration and the exchange of best practice among EU states is important. While several organisations are working on tracking discrimination, racism and xenophobia, there are only piecemeal attempts at keeping tabs on good integration practices. The last edition of the 'Handbook on Integration' is six years old and needs to be updated.

Integration requires a 'whole of society' approach. Canada's large-scale and ambitious immigration strategy has demonstrated that tools ranging from sports clubs to church and mosque-related activities have a powerful influence on the absorption of younger immigrants into the societies of host countries. The role of local authorities is especially important.

3. The EU Budget Should Ease and Spread The Costs of Mass Immigration

The immigration-related squabbling and finger-pointing that threatens the European project comes down, of course, to money. Last year's influx represented an immediate cost of €35bn.

That promise is being eclipsed by immediate budgetary strains in EU countries. German's authoritative Kiel Institute for the World Economy is therefore urging that 'the distribution of refugees would be far less controversial if the full fiscal cost of providing for them until they can earn their own living was borne by the EU budget.'

New financial instruments are urgently needed to address short-term costs, but there are few signs of this so far. The EU commission's move last autumn for a €1.7bn increase of 2015-16 spending on refugee costs, raising it to €9.2bn, will chiefly go on tightening borders to keep people out. Defusing tensions between EU governments by spreading the immediate burden more evenly has received little support.

4. EU Governments Must Speed Job-Seeking Immigrants Into Work

Economic migrants are far from being the burden that politicians and the media suggest. Although widely vilified as 'benefits scroungers', they predominantly come to Europe to find work.

Public opinion demands that native Europeans' jobs should be 'protected' from newcomers, whether refugees or job-seeking migrants, yet the truth is Europe's shrinking workforces are crying out for both categories to help restore much-needed economic dynamism. More publicity should be given to the stories of migrant entrepreneurs who are fostering the revitalization of impoverished urban neighbourhoods by creating jobs and prompting innovation in products and services. Migrant entrepreneurs account for 10% of overall self-employed business in Germany, 11% in France and an impressive 14% in Britain.

That process might well be speeded up if job-seeking immigrants were able to accept lower wages than native European workers. That idea, needless to say, is fervently opposed by trade unions and others who claim it would initiate a 'race to the bottom'. The contest seems unresolvable between those who urge the overall economic benefits of harnessing much-needed immigrant manpower and their opponents who say many decades of social progress would be threatened.

The arguments for quickly getting the newcomers into work as an overall economic boost are convincing. The public mood in the EU's Nordic countries has been swinging against refugees, but the IMF remains convinced of the benefits. 'A back-of-the-envelope calculation shows that real GDP in the average Nordic country will be about 2.5% higher by 2020 compared to a scenario in which there is no continued migration', it states in a mid-January report.

The question is how to overcome the difficulties of integrating newcomers into Europe's labour markets? The answers lie in the hands of governments. Lifting the bans in some countries on asylum-seekers' ability to find employment would be an obvious first step, as would ending some governments' insistence that employers pay a statutory minimum wage. But the argument that low-skilled immigrants need to price themselves into work is, as mentioned earlier in the boxed section of the introduction to this report, hotly contested.

In the case of immigrants with qualifications, EU countries should be taking a close look at the red tape surrounding their recognition of diplomas. It's a major problem, given that UNHCR has said that about half of the adult refugees from Syria have a university degree. The IMF echoed that when it reported that tertiary education amongst Syrian newcomers was close to the average for Germany.

The easiest way to encourage employers to take on job-seeking newcomers is by offering them wage subsidies. When Denmark tried out wage subsidy programmes for private employers, the time it took immigrants to land a job was cut by three to six months. In short, a thorough re-think of the taxes and benefits affecting refugees and migrants would pay handsome dividends.

5. The EU Should Contest the Fallacy that Migrants "Steal" European Jobs

It is one of the most stubbornly-held misconceptions that newcomers displace existing job holders by undercutting them and accepting lower wages. Economists have long derided the 'lump of labour fallacy' and its notion that a finite number of jobs have to be divided, with newcomers therefore 'stealing work' from native employees. Instead, migrants swell the workforce and help to expand the overall economy, but it's a message that has gained little traction with public opinion.

The IMF's analysts say plainly in their recent report on the refugee surge in Europe that this isn't a serious threat. They conclude that while the displacement effects on native workers are a major political concern, they are

likely to be short-lived and small. The IMF authors note that 'past experience with both economic and humanitarian immigration indicates that adverse effects on wages or employment are limited and temporary'.

It's up to governments and civil society leaders to hammer home this message. The IMF points out that far from hitting people in the pocket, it is countries like Austria, Germany and Sweden that have been the most successful in getting immigrants into work that are benefitting the most economically.

6. Authorities Should Help Immigrant Entrepreneurs Through Access to Credit

New businesses could do much to integrate the newcomers, and also serve the needs of immigrant communities that look set to grow rapidly over the years ahead. But immigrant entrepreneurs need far more support than they currently enjoy. On average, only 18% of microloans for small start-ups went to immigrants and ethnic minorities in 2013.

There's a host of barriers that obstruct immigrants' use of widely-available financial services. There are 'proof of residency' requirements along with language and cultural differences that make it hard for newcomers to open a bank account and obtain a credit or debit card. These are banal and easily-remedied handicaps that needlessly delay the integration process.

Some EU countries - notably the Netherlands, followed by Belgium - have pioneered the use of microloans to encourage enterepreneurial immigrants, and this should be highlighted and supported by the EU.

7. EU Governments Should Launch Ambitious and Coordinated Housing Drives

The sudden surge of refugees is laying bare housing shortages that had anyway been growing in a good many EU countries. Emergency housing is in itself a problem, but the much greater challenge is the longer term one of building affordable homes in a strategy that

Preventing Root Causes of Displacement

The world needs early warning and response systems to detect emerging tensions and promote reconciliation while good governance and the rule of law are strengthened in order to address the very causes of mass movements of refugees, said United Nations Development Programme (UNDP) Administrator Helen Clark.

Speaking at the United Nations Summit for Refugees and Migrants, Helen Clark also stressed the importance of improving data collection and analysis in order to better cope with the causes of displacement.

[…]

"Throughout human history, people have sought to better their lives through leaving their homes for places where prospects may be better. The root causes of large movements of people include flight from armed conflict and human rights violation, lack of good governance, poverty, marginalisation of communities and environmental degradation – including that exacerbated by climate change," she said at a round-table meeting at the UN summit.

At the moment, there are 21 million refugees around the world. Clark noted that the 2030 Agenda and the Sustainable Development Goals (SDGs) provides a framework for responding to large movements of people. She said that partnerships between governments, civil society, the private sector, the UN system and international financial institutions are necessary in order to respond.

"The international community should place conflict prevention and mediation at the center of international peace and security efforts. Early warning and response systems are needed for when tensions emerge and to foster reconciliation," Clark said.

"International support is needed to strengthen good governance and the rule of law, and to address structural inequalities. Promoting inclusive economic growth and sustainable livelihoods is critical for building peaceful and inclusive societies," she said.

[…]

"Early warnings and good governance crucial to preventing root causes of displacement: UNDP's Helen Clark," United Nations Development Programme (UNDP), September 19, 2016.

avoids the 'ghettoisation' of migrants while also ensuring that they are re-settled in areas with good employment prospects.

In Germany, the authorities are well aware of this need, even if the political climate has soured. Andrea Nahles, the federal labour minister, put the country's needs in a nutshell when she said: 'We have more than a million vacancies, with a need for qualified personnel. More than half of those (immigrants) who come to us are younger than 25, so this could really work out'.

But that awareness of the labour needs of Germany and other EU countries has yet to translate into action. Political sensitivities, combining no doubt with the difficulties of doing anything speedily in Europe, are blocking the way to housing drives that would also help to kick-start economic growth.

8. The EU Must Highlight Education as the Key to Migrants' Integration

The refugee crisis is not a passing phenomenon, and requires a long-term policy approach if it isn't to destabilize European society. It also offers a solution to the waning numbers of students in the education systems of EU countries.

Europe's declining birthrate threatens the viability of establishments ranging from kindergartens to universities. Students in Germany were slated to dwindle by 10% by 2025, but now the immigrant influx will help redress that shrinkage.

This still leaves the problem of how to avoid under-performing schools that compound the difficulties of integrating immigrant communities. The record so far in many parts of Europe is discouraging, with children of ethic minorities tending to score much lower than the average. Innovative schemes in the Netherlands and France, however, which are geared specifically to the integration of second-generation migrants are proving successful—and should be replicated in other countries.

No one can doubt, though, that the children of the refugee crisis will be crucial to ageing Europe's future. Their parents may not be so easily assimilated into European society, but hey themselves are a crucially important asset and should be recognized as such. The emphasis at the moment appears to be on anti-radicalisation measures. While these are important, more attention should be paid on the wider array of policies needed to ensure a more successful integration of young people.

9. EU Governments Should Offer Tax Incentives to 'Sponsors' of Immigrants

Rather than create more layers of law governing access to benefits, European governments would do better to introduce tax relief for individuals, companies and organisations capable of sponsoring newcomers.

The costs involved in taking in immigrants are already a disincentive for many. But housing and job opportunities could be greatly increased if financial inducements were to complement the sympathy that Europeans have already shown for the plight of refugees.

Simple across-the-board tax rebates for companies offering employment and individuals making accommodation available would do much to relieve the strain on local authorities. It is an approach that could usefully be incorporated into existing Corporate Social Responsibility (CSR) programmes.

10. The EU Should Present Migration as Part of the Solution to its Looming Pension Crisis

The crude 'gee-whiz' statistic increasingly used by those policy analysts concerned with the ageing of Europe is that by mid-century the present ration of one pensioner for every four workers will have shrunk to one or two. With today's pension systems already under severe pressure, that's an alarming prospect.

The European Commission last year published a study of the likely effects of ageing on pensions, and found that stemming the flow of immigrants would substantially raise pension costs. It calculated that each yearly reduction of 210,000 people in the numbers of newcomers over the next 15 years would translate into higher pension costs amounting to 0.1% of GDP.

'Countries receiving the largest inflows (of refugees),' the EU report said, 'would experience the strongest reduction in pension outlays', adding that they would also cut health service and old age care costs.

[…]

Send Development Aid, Not Weapons

Jeffrey D. Sachs

In the following viewpoint, Jeffrey D. Sachs criticizes America's current foreign policies. He says that the first step in solving the refugee crisis is to stop the conflicts – largely caused by US policies – that are creating refugees. He recommends focusing on promoting sustainable development in other countries, rather than using military intervention. He notes that this development must take into account climate change or else risk even greater numbers of refugees in the future. Jeffrey D. Sachs is an American economist and professor at Columbia University.

As you read, consider the following questions:

1. What has been the effect of US attempts to overthrow leaders in Middle Eastern countries, according to the author?
2. How does the amount of money the US spends on foreign development assistance compare to the amount it spends on the military?
3. How might global warming affect the number of refugees and migrants?

I n Europe and the United States, immigration is the number one political issue. Passions are high, dangerously so. The stakes are

"A three-point solution to the migrant crisis," by Jeffrey D. Sachs, The Boston Globe, March 15, 2016. Reprinted by permission.

high as well. Migrants are risking their lives, and dying, to escape from violence, poverty, and joblessness. How can we reconcile the flood of migrants and the stiff backlash in the receiving societies?

I propose a three-part approach. The first is to stop the conflicts that are currently causing millions of refugees to flee their homes. The second is to promote long-term economic development in the countries migrants are fleeing. The third is to adjust global policies to enshrine the freedom to migrate while also enabling societies to limit migration to moderate and manageable rates.

Two conflict zones in particular, the Middle East and Central America, account for the recent surge of refugees to Europe and the United States, respectively. In both regions, an urgently needed change of US foreign policy could staunch this flow. Sadly, both regions have instead been destabilized by misguided US policies.

The Middle East conflicts are US wars of choice. The three largest conflicts in the region, Iraq (2003-present), Libya (2011-present), and Syria (2011-present) reflect the repeated US resort to violent "regime change," starting with the toppling of Iraq's Saddam Hussein, and continuing with the overthrow of Libya's Moammar Khadafy and, most recently, the attempted overthrow of Syria's Bashar al-Assad. In all three cases, the result has been open-ended conflict and the rise of violent jihadists. As a result, millions of refugees have been crossing the Mediterranean into Europe from departure points mainly in Turkey and Libya.

In Central America, as in the Middle East, lame-brained CIA schemes — such as the 1980s contra wars, the 2004 Haiti coup against Jean-Bertrand Aristide, and the 2009 Honduran coup against Manuel Zalaya — have stoked violence and created pervasive instability. In addition, the so-called US war on drugs, fought in many parts of Latin America, has fomented massive violence. An American public health crisis — the epidemic use of opiates — has been transmuted into open war south of the US border.

Both the Middle East and Central America demonstrate a compelling case for demilitarizing US foreign policy. Ending covert

CIA operations in the Middle East, Central America, and Africa would immediately reduce the displacement of populations and flow of refugees. Facing the opiate epidemic for what it really is — a public health challenge caused by massive social inequalities and desperation within US communities — would stop the Latin American drug wars, save lives, and enable Central Americans to live in peace while remaining in their own countries.

Of course, even without the CIA wars of choice and the misguided war on drugs, millions of people around the world will still want to migrate to the United States and Europe in search of jobs, higher living standards, and social benefits. They will also come to escape from environmental degradation and the dislocations caused by global warming.

The correct response is to promote sustainable development in countries of large-scale out-migration. People will want to remain in their homelands if they see a viable future for their children. The good news is that sustainable development is feasible, and promoting it would be much cheaper for the United States and Europe than pursuing more failed wars, which have already cost the US trillions of dollars in the Middle East alone in the past 15 years.

Yet US foreign policy is disastrously imbalanced: US military outlays outrun development assistance by roughly 25 to 1. Or to put it another way, our total aid budget is equal to around two weeks of Pentagon spending. The reason is obvious. Washington politicians salivate over each new taxpayer-subsidized weapons sale, which brings in its wake new campaign contributions and jobs for recycled politicians. Fighting disease, illiteracy, and poverty simply doesn't provide the D.C. political class with the same returns.

Looking ahead, the migration pressures will intensify unless the world acts to slow, and soon to stop, human-made global warming. If we fail to fulfill the climate commitments made last December in Paris, many places in the world will become less habitable and, for some, even uninhabitable. Global warming causes declining food yields in the tropics; intensifying droughts in the dry lands of North Africa and the Middle East; an expanded transmission zone of tropical diseases; more intense cyclones in Southeast Asia; and rising sea levels and flooding in coastal regions.

In addition to ending useless wars and promoting sustainable development, the third part of migration policy should be to make the world safe for diversity and for ongoing migration. Every one of us is from a migrant family. Every one of us has ancestors, if not our selves, who have been "strangers in a strange land." The reasons for migration will continue to be powerful and diverse in the future. Our global norms and policies should respect the human right to migrate, albeit within reasonable limits.

Countries are certainly right to police their borders, but at the same time should keep an open door for moderate and manageable rates of in-migration. No country should be allowed to slam its doors shut (and none would be wise to do so, and thereby lose the benefits of diversity). And while countries may be justified in limiting some social benefits to new migrants (to keep fiscal costs manageable and to limit incentives for excessive migrant inflows), the US and other countries should ensure that migrant children receive the health care, schooling, and nutrition they need for their healthy development.

In short, migration is not about building high walls but about creating a world in which people can live securely and prosperously in their own homelands, while still enjoying the freedom to migrate for personal reasons rather than in desperation. By viewing the migration crisis in a more holistic way we will find true and lasting solutions rather than the demagogic ones now widely on offer.

Technology Provides Answers

Alina O'Keeffe and Dan Swann

In the following excerpted viewpoint, Alina O'Keeffe and Dan Swann argue that technology has a major role to play in humanitarian aid. This report discusses several challenges that can be addressed by technology, including gathering data and communicating with people in need. During disasters, basic resources such as light and safe water can be difficult to supply. Recent inventions address these issues or help provide medical supplies, sanitation, housing, and food. Alina O'Keeffe and Dan Swann are involved with the Aid and International Development Forum, which addresses disaster relief.

As you read, consider the following questions:

1. How does technology help people communicate during disasters and relief efforts?
2. Why do medical providers working in disaster relief need heating and refrigeration?
3. How do solar lights benefit refugees in camps?

Humanitarian stakeholders face a number of interconnected current or emerging challenges, including climate change, ever-growing refugee crisis, as well as water scarcity and food insecurity. Science and technological innovations play a critical

"Inspiring Solutions That Save Lives & Support Development – 2016 Edition," published at http://www.aidforum.org/disaster-relief/inspiring-solutions-that-save-lives-support-development-2016-edition by Alina O'Keeffe, Aid & International Development Forum (AID) and Dan Swann, Technology Exchange Lab, April 07, 2016. Reprinted by permission.

role in contributing to effective aid delivery and enabling efficient disaster response and development programmes.

As part of the annual update of the guide to "Solutions That Save Lives & Support Development", the Aid and International Development Forum (AIDF) together with the Technology Exchange Lab have researched latest technologies and innovations, which can help humanitarian actors to mitigate the future implications of these challenges.

With over 300 solutions nominated by NGOs, local governments, UN agencies and the private sector working in 58 different countries, the guide offers an updated list of cutting-edge technologies and products which support Sustainable Development Goals, aid delivery and disaster relief efforts across the globe.

[…]

Data Collection, Geographic Information Systems (GIS) and Mapping

From the perspective of the Post-2015 Development Agenda, the data revolution presents an opportunity of transformation towards a more sustainable society. Data can be used not only for optimisation, but also to sense the needs of the people more accurately in real time and connect better with communities. Furthermore, data can be used to improve the representativeness and transparency in policy making.

Inspired by the data revolution and working towards Sustainable Development Goals, itdData, initiated by Innovation and Technology for Development Centre at the Technical University of Madrid, designs Big Data projects for social innovation and development, helping to improve interactions between actors in the society.

Aeryon Labs boasts the SkyRanger, an unmanned aerial vehicle (UAV) solution for aerial mapping and search, and recover operations. It has been tested and proven in harsh environments and challenging conditions and requires very little training for new operators.

Project NOAH is a website that consolidates geospatial data to help develop near real-time disaster management systems for the Philippines. The project lets end-users to use LIDAR data to view high resolution topographic data as a base map and as DEM (digital elevation model) for use in hazards modelling and other purposes.

The Myanmar Information Management Unit is an information management service, a sort of "one-stop shop" for data, maps and other resources needed by government agencies, NGOs, the UN, and others trying to implement humanitarians and development projects.

Akvo is a not-for-profit foundation that creates open source, internet and mobile software and sensors. Akvo helps organisations collect, analyse, and share data, therein helping to make development and governance more transparent.

UltiSat is a global provider of secure, reliable satellite communications networks for military and government entities, telcos, service providers, IGOs, and enterprises. It recently launched UlitNet, a comprehensive portfolio that integrates satellite, wireless and information security products and services. UltiNet enables high value, SLA-based, C and/or Ku-band connectivity to end users in remote and harsh territories.

Planet Labs operate the largest constellation of earth-imaging satellites, which collect data to support aid delivery after natural disasters, amongst other applications. Planet Labs offers global imagery to empower informed and meaningful stewardship of our planet.

Information and Communication Technologies (ICT)

As digital technology is constantly evolving, Information and Communication Technologies (ICT) play significant role in improving the quality and efficiency of humanitarian aid and development work. Humanitarian actors rely on tools that foster effective communication in order to support effective programming and satisfy the need for information, which exists amongst those affected by humanitarian disasters.

Organisations can use the VOTO mobile phone notification and survey system to promote healthy behaviours via voice messages or SMS. Users can promote healthy behaviours or educational information, announce meetings, and share local news.

UNICEF Innovation in partnership with Nyaruka, developed RapidPro, which allows to connect directly with a user on their mobile phone over SMS, voice, or social media without the help of a software developer. From youth engagement programmes like U-Report to education monitoring systems like EduTrac, RapidPro has become UNICEF's common platform for developing and sharing mobile services that can be adapted for different contexts and sectors.

Similar to RapidPro, U-Report is designed to empower people in developing countries to speak out on issues in their communities. Users can reply to SMS polls and alerts every week, thereby giving administrators an immediate snapshot of the situation. As a large-scale SMS tool available in 21 countries, operationalisation of U-Report in an emergency is now central to UNICEF disaster Risk Reduction and Response measures.

Thuraya, a mobile satellite communication company, now offers SatSleeve, a simple and user-friendly way to convert an iPhone into a satellite smartphone. Satellite mode offers users the ability to make calls, check email, and more in places where there is no terrestrial network.

Global Xpress, Inmarsat's new global high-speed broadband service, enables aid and NGO organisations to deliver fast reliable broadband internet for first responder teams, no matter where they're deployed.

Helios Worker Safety provides a rugged cell phone with push-to-talk communication and SOS alarm button. Features include group messaging, location, dispatch service, and a SOS button. It works off any data connection.

The ONE Solution from RedRose is a complete programme management system that provides end-to-end solutions for humanitarian agencies. NGOs can register beneficiaries; mobilise cash transfers, DIK's, and voucher programming; and conduct reporting and monitoring.

Disaster Response

Volatility, uncertainty, complexity and ambiguity - disasters affect millions of people each year around the global. Responses and logistics, in particular, remain inefficient for a number of reasons.

Field Ready aims to effectively develop products and services for people in developing countries and disaster areas. Professionals from Silicon Valley have contributed their expertise in humanitarian work, technology, design, and engineering in order to provide practical and unique solutions that help people in need.

When a humanitarian crisis or natural disaster strikes, the need for natural resources such as water and light is vital to saving lives. To ensure that demand is met, Business Connect has established a network of suppliers that will enable the company to provide critical assistance when timing is crucial.

The S.E.A. Group (website under construction - see announcement) is comprised of six enterprises from Cordoba dedicated to the production and provision of supplies and services in the field of humanitarian aid, emergencies and natural disasters. These enterprises are engaged in: wildfire suppression and rescue equipment; the design and development of flow measurement and control equipment; tailored early warning products and services for predicting floods and wildfires; rapid deployment solutions; telecommunications infrastructure and water treatment units; special vehicles equipment; and more.

Recent partnership between Hexagon's incident management software, Intergraph Computer-Aided Dispatch (I/CAD), and TomTom helps optimise emergency response performance in countries, including Australia, India and South Korea. TomTom's map and traffic data in combination with I/CAD will help increase dispatching accuracy and reduce response times to incidents and emergencies in the Asia-Pacific region.

Healthcare & Medical Equipment

According to World Health Organization (WHO), dengue is the fastest growing mosquito-borne disease in the world today, causing nearly 400 million infections annually. Worldwide, the annual cost of dengue disease control effort is estimated at US$ 8.9 billion. The suffering and economic impact caused by this disease do not only affect at public health and societal level but also directly at individuals and families.

After 20 years of research and development and close collaborations with the global dengue scientific and public health communities, Sanofi Pasteur is making the world's first dengue vaccine available. As a part of an integrated approach for effective control of the disease, this vaccine could be a game changer, contributing to the achievement of the WHO objectives to reduce worldwide dengue morbidity and mortality by 25% and 50% respectively by 2020.

Royal Philips and the Sijunjung Regency in West Sumatra, Indonesia, have developed a full-scale implementation of Philips' Mobile Obstetrics Monitoring (MOM) service in the region following a successful pilot programme. This scalable smartphone-based digital health service is designed to identify mothers-to-be who are at high risk of pregnancy-related complications and help reduce maternal mortality rates. The MOM solution enables midwives in remote locations to share vital measurements, observational data and mobile ultrasound images with obstetricians and gynaecologists in the country's larger hospitals and collaborate with them for improved decision making during pregnancy.

HemoCue point-of-care testing systems give fast and accurate anaemia screening, which can be advantageous during health consultations and in emergency situations. In particular, HemoCue® Hb 201 DM System improves the administrative workflow and safeguards patient testing and data, with data management in Hb point-of-care testing.

InStove Autoclaves are solid-fuel devices for medical equipment sterilisation. It has been used in several countries, including post-earthquake Nepal and in over 60 clinics throughout the Democratic Republic of the Congo. It is a safe, efficient, and low-cost way to sterilise medical supplies and bio-hazardous waste. Plus, it can double as a biomass cook stove, now rated as one of the cleanest, safest and most efficient of its kind. The Autoclave system has been listed by the WHO in their 2014 Compendium of Innovative Health Technologies for Low-Resource settings.

SATMED is dedicated to providing open-access e-Health and m-Health tools and services to assist non-governmental organisations, hospitals, medical universities and other health care providers active in resource-poor areas. SATMED tools and services support and facilitate work and projects in the area of e-care, e-learning, e-surveillance, e-health management and e-health financing.

B Medical Systems medical refrigeration equipment is used for large-scale vaccination programs in emerging markets. This year the company will be launching a series of new products developed specifically for the cold chain of vaccines.

Wash

AFRIpads Menstrual Kits are reusable sanitary pads designed to provide superior feminine hygiene protection and comfort. Made from high-performance textiles, the kits provide effective protection for 12+ months (menstrual cycles), making them a cost-effective and eco-friendly solution. The design is an "all-in-one" pad that buttons securely into a pair of underwear.

Real Relief Way water filter has been designed for use in developing countries and disaster areas, where access to clean drinking water is particularly important.

Flexigester System is the first rapid deployment anaerobic digestion system with a capacity to process over ten tons of sanitation waste, created by Butyl Products.

Ultrafiltration Systems and Reverse Osmosis Systems are highly mobile water filtration and treatment equipment designed by Kärcher Futuretech. It consumes little energy and can be broken down into portable, individual modules for transportation to remote rural areas with an aim to provide good quality drinking water in a sufficient quantity wherever needed.

Envirosan creates environmentally friendly sanitation solutions. Using technologically advanced machines and techniques, Envirosan is able to provide a comprehensive range of plastic injection moulded sanitation systems and solutions, specialising in waterless sanitary products.

The DayOne Waterbag™ from Day One Response is a 10-liter (2.5 gallon) family-sized water bag purification device with integrated filter and backpack straps. The Waterbag provides all four of the functions needed to treat and safely store drinking water: collection, transportation, treatment, and hygienic storage. It is a compact solution designed for use in emergency situations, and natural disasters where the drinking water supply has been depleted or is of unknown quality.

AquaResearch set out to design a water treatment system that would meet the extreme needs of individuals and families in developing countries. Enter the H2gO Purifier, a rugged and low-cost, solar-powered handheld device that uses only salt to purify water.

The Fieldtrate Lite from WaterRoam, is a lightweight, point-of-use, instant microbiological water purifier that can provide instant access to clean and safe drinking water. It has a flow rate of 6-9 L/h which can provide for a household (5-7 people) microbiologically clean drinking water for up to 3-5 years. Fieldtrate Lite is capable of removing bacteria, pathogens and of protozoan parasites without any electrical power.

Agriculture, Food & Nutrition

Agriculture makes the living of millions of family farmers and their respective communities. The agricultural performance affects food security. ICT enable traceability that is the first step to get organic labelling and thus give access to higher sales prices.

Over the last few years, the cloud has significantly changed how organisations utilise software and there is no secret why cloud has ascended into the mainstream of business technology. Agraria, a company dedicated to the implementation and operation of a services platform based on SAP HANA Cloud, runs the Ivory Coast Rural Market Place, which is part of the wider eAgri project by the Ivory Coast Government. The initiative aims to recruit one million small farmers as part of the country's 2020 objective to implement transformational e-government services. Such solutions are an integral and crucial enabler for innovation and development in Africa, as recognised at the recent AIDF Africa Summit 2016.

NutriMyanmar, a programme run by a French non-profit association GRET, which supports a local business to design, market and promote breast milk supplement for young children (6-23 months) with an aim to fight child malnutrition in two pilot areas of urban and rural Myanmar.

In the Philippines, the Department of Science Technology is establishing Complementary Food Production (CFP) facilities as part of its Malnutrition Reduction Program, an initiative created to address the prevalence of under nutrition among children from 6 months to 3 years old. The CFP facilities are being set up in partnership with local government units in order to use technologies to continuously produce nutritious baby food blends and snack foods made from rice, mongo, sesame, and other locally available raw materials. These facilities and technologies enable production of complementary foods readily available for feeding programmes and emergency situations, as well as for market distribution.

Global Food Exchange offers a fleet of products and services needed for basic survival following natural disasters and other forms of crises. It offers four "vaults," specialised packages of goods and services designed for rapid deployment to meet critical needs related to food, clean water, and shelter.

SlowFood International has a three-pronged mission: to prevent the disappearance of local food cultures and traditions; to counteract the rise of fast life; and to combat people's dwindling interest in the food they eat, in where it comes from, and how our food choices affect the world around us. A grassroots movement now in 160 countries, Slow Food engages in biodiversity projects, spurs celebratory events to draw attention to local foods, and builds networks to connect people passionate about changing food systems.

A new livestock insurance product, run by the Kenya-based International Livestock Research Institute (ILRI), uses satellite imagery to determine forage availability and offers payouts when there is lack of rain in order to protect herders income against drought. The index-based insurance programme is funded by the British, U.S. and Australian governments and the European Union. With assistance from Kenya's Ministry of Agriculture, it subsidised five tropical livestock units (TLUs) for free for poor households, who cannot afford insurance premiums.

Human-powered treadle pump is one of the low-cost technologies used by farmers to irrigate land. Such pumps, advanced by iDE Bangladesh supply chain development programmes, have been introduced in Burkina Faso, Ethiopia, Ghana, Mozambique and Zambia following their success in Bangladesh.

Energy Supply

Concentrating solar dishes from A Better Focus are inexpensive devices for solar cooking, water purification, and heat storage. These cookers generate a higher level of heat energy, though the cost of materials is relatively low. The designer is willing to train local residents in the manufacture and implementation of these dishes.

The Safe Access to Fuel and Energy (SAFE) Humanitarian Working Group aims to provide refugees with crucial access to energy for lighting and powering. Solar lighting devices make it safer for people to navigate camps at night, and they enable them to continue studying or working after dark. Mini-grids can provide electricity for crucial camp functions such as security, lighting, communication, water pumping, and waste management.

In Africa, "One Lamp, One Child" project, initiated by a Taiwanese company, Speedtech Energy, equipped children with Solar Reading Lights in order to improve their education.

The Global Alliance for Clean Cookstoves recognised that food distributed by humanitarian agencies is typically dry and energy dense; often, it must be cooked for long periods of time before it can be eaten. Without clean and efficient cook stoves, many families rely on solid fuels such as wood or charcoal for cooking, which create smoky fires that damage respiratory health. Providing clean cook stoves and alternative fuels to crisis affected populations can save lives and support development.

AidGear designs portable power and water purification systems for disaster responders and military units - lightweight (less than 70lbs) and efficient (treat water at 2 gallons/minute) solutions for mobile teams.

Solar-powered lanterns, by Renewit, use the latest LED technology to deliver high powered, bright lasting white light. A Hong Kong based design and manufacturing company also offers Home Power Stations to enable a complete lifestyle change in the home with the ability to power lighting, radios, TV and Fridges.

Logistics, Shipping & Aid Delivery

ReliefOps.Ph is a web-based decision support tool for better logistics during disaster relief and rescue operations. Created by Reinabelle Reyes, Lecturer at the Department of Physics and Department of Information Systems and Computer Science Ateneo de Manila University or "The Filipina who proved Einstein right", it contributes to the government's research and development initiatives to address the major challenges in disaster risk reduction and management facing Philippines.

UPS offers a range of shipping solutions designed specifically for temperature sensitive or perishable pharmaceuticals with an aim to tackle supply shortages and adverse impact on beneficiaries' health as a result. Special packaging, refrigerated trucks, air and ocean, cargo and cryogenic shipping containers as well as constant monitoring ensure that shipments stay within specified temperatures throughout the journeys. UPS Order Watch®, enabled by the cloud-based technology platform, allows tighter connectivity and efficient supply chain management to decrease lead times and improve reliable fulfillment.

Crown Agents is a non-profit social enterprise with almost 200 years' experience in supply and logistics. In this area its key competence is in end to end solutions including last miles solutions. Greenshields Cowie, Crown Agents' wholly owned logistics and freight forwarding operation, moved 2,111 tonnes of essential aid into the country, from items required for the construction the six Ebola Treatment Centres to personal protective equipment and life-saving medicines. Crown Agents provides similar solutions for crises in Iraq, South Sudan and Syria, providing capacity building to local companies and customs.

Emergency Logistics Team is setting out to develop and deliver a suite of Humanitarian & Emergency Logistics (H&EL) training programmes. ELT has already worked with one midsize UK INGO, Health Poverty Action. Bringing such an organisation's procurement functions more in line with modern professional operations could give them the opportunity to bid for larger funds from donors, in turn giving them more autonomy in the running of their day to day operations.

Humanitarian Logistics Association promotes and supports professional development initiatives within the global humanitarian logistics community of practice. It acts as a neutral interface to leverage knowledge, information and capability across humanitarian organisations.

The American Logistics Aid Network (ALAN) helps locate and move goods from suppliers to affected communities rapidly and efficiently by comprising hundreds of supply-chain businesses who are prepared to respond in the event of disasters. ALAN's web portal serves as a clearinghouse for essential supplies, goods, and services during times of crisis, where relief organisations post urgent needs on the portal, from requests for local warehouse space to advice on how to best move products into position.

The SPACCER lifting system provides an easy and fast method for lifting vehicle's front and/or rear by up to 48mm. The suspension lift kits are custom-made for each individual vehicle type thus providing availability for all makes and models.

Shelter & Temporary Housing

The Aussie Mozzie Tube is a lightweight, portable, and vermin proof personal sleeping capsule. It is available via self-manufacturing to help smaller communities, states and countries to prepare before disaster strikes and to provide the first line of defence following disaster. The Aussie Mozzie Tube can be manufactured using lightweight materials, basic skills and domestic sewing machines.

The winterHYDE from billionBricks is a life-saving, fully insulated, lightweight shelter designed to provide privacy and to protect a family as large as five from the cold.

Tiguri devised the Tiguri Green Village, a fully integrated way to build a connected, sustainable community with access to electricity, clean drinking water, and a self-contained waste processing system. It is designed to provide marginalised groups with access to shelter, sanitation, and safety, easily and efficiently.

NRS Relief Shelter Repair Tool Kit is specifically designed for distribution in the aftermath of a disaster when shelter capacities have been affected. The 'one kit per family' includes rope, handsaw, various nails, machete, shovel, hoe, tire wire, claw hammer, polyethylene bag and a cardboard fold, all to ICRC/IFRC Standard.

Community Engagement

Rappler is a social news network for stories that may inspire community engagement and for digitally fueled actions for social change. Following disasters, Rappler provides crowd sourced information, as well as link requests for assistance to the appropriate agencies and for private sector support.

Heroic Improvisation helps communities by creating theatre improvisation workshops in order to catalyse their abilities to respond to disaster and other high-stakes events. Such exercises enable participants to practice the skills of individual awareness, leadership focus, and coordinated action that are required in difficult situations.

World Vision International is helping to establish community-managed Savings Groups. World Vision Savings Groups are appropriate mechanisms that can be integrated with other humanitarian responses to support livelihoods self-recovery, strengthening, promotion and resilience building. The group mechanism is a platform that can be used for disseminating early warning and preparedness information and are a base for social capital that can be drawn upon during and after disasters.

Training and Education

MSD provides solutions for not-for profit organisations that help with capacity building on good governance, transparency, and accountability through Organisational Development of Inspiring Culture. MSD includes self-assessment, blended training courses, coaching packages, independent certificates, and awarding for best practice organisations. This solution can be used by NGOs, social investor, donors and government to evaluate and build capacity for NGOs.

Long-Term Solutions Mean Sharing the Burden

United Nations

In the following excerpted viewpoint, the United Nations calls for new solutions to help people displaced by conflict. Because the number of refugees is rising and the number of time they spend displaced is lengthening, solutions must be long-term. The authors argue that the international community should share the burden more equally, taking into account the money host countries spend to support refugees. Refugees should be allowed to take employment so they can become self-reliant, and refugee children must be educated.

As you read, consider the following questions:

1. How long do people displaced by conflict usually spend living in displacement?
2. How does the financial cost of educating refugee children compare to not educating them?
3. Does this report recommend increasing or decreasing the number of countries that offer resettlement to refugees?

The number of people enduring protracted displacement is on the rise. More people today are displaced by conflict and violence than at any time since 1945, with nearly 60 million people by the end of 2014. Worldwide there were 19.5 million refugees, 38.2 million were displaced inside their own countries, and 1.8 million people were awaiting the outcome of claims for asylum. In 2014 alone, 13.9 million people became newly displaced – four times the number of the previous year.[275] The average length of time a person lives in displacement is now over 17 years. New solutions are urgently needed to generate hope and more durable solutions for millions of women, men and children.

There was a strong call from the WHS consultations for the international community to:

- recognize the massive contribution made by host countries and support them with long term investment, including in infrastructure and services;
- shift approaches to improve refugee resilience and self-reliance;
- improve assistance to host communities, reducing resentment and conflict;
- protect, assist and find durable solutions for internally displaced people;
- address the humanitarian dimensions of migrant and refugee movements by reinforcing life-saving efforts and through commitments to protect and promote the human rights of all people on the move.

Create a Shift in Approach to Refugees

With a constant rise in numbers of refugees, and in the duration of their displacement, the consultations called for a fundamental shift in how refugees are supported. Long-term predictable investments should support host communities and refugees to mutual benefit, promote dignity and self-reliance through livelihood opportunities, and create more equitable arrangements for third country resettlement.

The consultations called for a fundamental shift in how refugees are supported, including for the global community to recognize the global public good that refugee hosting countries provide, for

Dignified and safe shelter for refugee camps[278]

Better Shelter, a Swedish social enterprise, designs safe and robust shelters for refugees across the world. Such products are an important evolution in emergency shelter, bringing dignity and safety to refugees in some of the world's most insecure places. At the center of the project is the idea of democratic design. Technical testing, pilot and field trials, and feedback workshops bring refugees into the design process, ensuring their practical, social and cultural concerns are heard and integrated in the shelters' design. The shelters are now being used in Ethiopia, Iraq and Nepal. These shelters can be more than homes: through use as buildings such as health clinics, women's centers, and children's play spaces, they can meet the many needs of those displaced from their homes.

long-term predictable investments to be made to support both refugees and host communities, and more equitable arrangements for third country resettlement. The consultations also called for new national and regional legal frameworks to fill gaps in the assistance and protection of internally displaced persons.

As the number of refugees surges, their displacement lengthens, and patterns change from rural camps to living in urban areas, the consultations called strongly for a more equitable sharing by countries globally in hosting refugees and for improved support for this. There was a call for the international community to recognize the global public good that refugee hosting countries provide, and the considerable cost they bear. The financial contribution of Turkey in hosting Syrian refugees was estimated to be $1.6bn in 2013,[276] which would make Turkey the third largest humanitarian donor by volume.[277] However, the contribution of hosting states is not considered part of humanitarian finance, obscuring the extent of their contribution.

To remedy this problem, a first step would be to establish a methodology for determining these costs and contributions, and ensuring that finance tracking mechanisms include them. A next step would be for the global community to provide predictable, long-term development investment to host countries from the start of a crisis to help minimize the impact and support stability.

Consultations also called for a shift in approach, away from policies of encampment and blocks to self-reliance and employment schemes. Some agencies are already making efforts in this direction, including UNHCR through its 2014 Policy on Alternatives to Camps. A second shift would improve the balance between assistance to refugees and to their host communities, reducing the resentment, tensions and violence described by Syrian refugees in Lebanon and Jordan.[279] Examples include investment to upgrade local infrastructure and basic services. This is also more cost effective than creating a parallel system of infrastructure and services for refugees, as is often the case if they are placed in camps.

Proposals from WHS Middle East and North Africa

- International community to more equitably share the burden of hosting refugees and to provide greater support to impacted host countries and communities, including efforts to build, upgrade and expand on national infrastructure and service delivery to displaced and host populations.

- Countries that are dependent on labour migration in the region should to provide refugees with temporary residencies and employment opportunities.

- All stakeholders should improve opportunities for durable solutions for displaced populations, such as developing a fixed quota for third country resettlement and supporting voluntary return under appropriate circumstances.

A shift in approach is starting to take place, sparked by the Syria crisis. Turkey, Jordan, and other countries are shifting away from camps, giving refugees the right to work, and absorbing them into their education system (see box 13). Other countries, such as Ghana and the Islamic Republic of Iran, include refugees in their

Box 13: Option for refugee education

One option to explore would be to reimburse governments for educating refugees within national educational systems. Available data indicates that the cost of emergency education ranges from 1.5 times the cost to the national system (Jordan, ages 5-11) to 5.3 times the cost (Lebanon, ages 12-17). Estimates of the cost of not schooling children show long-term impacts of billions of dollars and percentage points of GDP, reinforcing the economic value of educating all children. This proposal reflects the strategy that Turkey has largely adopted, at significant cost, in mainstreaming Syrian refugees into their existing education systems.[282] Doing the same with refugees worldwide, and helping governments to bear the costs, would provide education systems with additional investment and arguably help to reduce marginalization of an already vulnerable group. It could also, very quickly, help to ensure that generations do not get lost, reducing the risks of long term poverty and instability.[283]

national health insurance systems.[280] The value of an approach in which humanitarian and development actors enhance the capacity of national and local authorities to provide services to both displaced and host communities can also be seen in Cameroon, Niger and Tanzania. Hosting countries may be able to provide access to jobs and services for refugees in return for increased external investment. There is also the potential to set minimum targets for specific issues, such as ensuring that no displaced child should lose a month of education.[281]

Consultations also noted the need to hasten durable solutions.[284] UNHCR has stated starkly: "Solutions to situations of long-term displacement are desperately needed. It is unacceptable that tens of millions of persons are forced to live in limbo for years, even for decades."[285] Compared to the 1990s, when large numbers of displaced people were able to return home, declining numbers have been able to. As a result UNHCR has called upon the Summit to commit to three actions.

Implementing durable solutions[286]

1. Increase opportunities for voluntary and sustainable repatriation by (a) engaging in conflict recovery, peacebuilding and other related activities; and by (b) supporting sustainable development in countries or areas of return.

2. Increase opportunities for local integration, including by (a) making the evidence-based case for policies supportive of integration; and by (b) increasing international support to countries that commit to allowing the long-term displaced to integrate permanently.

3. Expand opportunities for (a) refugee resettlement by increasing the number of countries that offer resettlement and the number of places offered; and for (b) labour mobility and non-traditional pathways to solutions for all persons of concern.

Proposals from the Consultations

- To address the disproportionate degree to which certain countries host refugees, the international community must ensure more equitable sharing by providing support to and resettling people affected by protracted crises. Sustainable return and reintegration remains the most preferred durable solution. Where necessary and appropriate, this should be facilitated, including by enhancing investments in countries of origin to close development gaps that may hinder achievement of this durable solution." – WHS South and Central Asia, chair's summary

- Recognizing the needs of displaced people, including for durable solutions, and the burden placed on host governments and communities, there was a call for increased burden sharing of hosting refugees by the international community and the need to ensure a holistic approach to the management of crises, including planning for future displacement. Actors should address the needs of host

Innovation starting with communities[287]

Refugees' engagement in innovation in Uganda is often enabled by their ability to understand the local markets. In many refugee settlements and camps, existing infrastructure and services fail to fully meet the demand of those living inside. Because of the limited water supply, poor road networks and transportation services, lack of adequate health care and education, and no formal provision of electricity, there are significant gaps between the market levels of demand and supply that leaves space for innovative individuals to provide alternatives. In many cases, the innovators are explicitly attempting to address these gaps in available public goods and services as a way of benefiting their wider communities.

   In the Nakivale settlement in Uganda, the largest milling plant in the settlement – made up of five milling machines – turns refugee farmers' maize into flour. This milling plant, owned by a Rwandan refugee, is unique among others in the settlement because of the large scale of the business, which employs five other refugees as staff. The size of this milling operation meant that during 2013, when a new influx of Congolese refugees entered Nakivale, the owner of the plants milled maize for the World Food Programme to meet increased demand for food.

   communities in response planning and use humanitarian and development approaches, in line with national and local priorities. Development interventions should come at an early stage and include support to the local economy and making investments in basic services and infrastructure that benefit both the displaced and their hosts." – WHS Middle East and North Africa, co-chairs' summary

- The international community should support host countries by exploring a basic international social protection package/ fund for long-term refugees, including risk-financing mechanisms to cover health insurance, education and vocational training, livelihood grants, and other areas." – WHS South and Central Asia, chair's summary

- Scale up durable solutions for internally displaced and refugee populations, including the option of early integration into host communities and building the necessary local capacity to enable this." – WHS Eastern and Southern Africa, cochairs' summary

- Call for early and increased development investment in addressing protracted displacement." – WHS Europe and Others, cochairs' summary

- Establish a forum of experts that convenes periodically for particular protracted crises, mandated to evaluate the extent to which donors and humanitarian and development actors are effectively building resilience." – WHS Middle East and North Africa, final report

- Participants called for the scaling up of efficient and coordinated cash-based programming to provide people with greater choice and for including temporary employment opportunities as part of response programming. These were deemed necessary to ensure service delivery that preserves the dignity of displaced people. When appropriate, priority should be given to voluntary return programs." – WHS Middle East and North Africa, co-chairs' summary

[…]

Endnotes

275 UNHCR, *Global Trends Forced Displacement in 2014* (Geneva, UNHCR, 2015).

276 Turkish Cooperation and Coordination Agency, *Turkish Development Assistance Report 2013* (Ankara, Turkish Cooperation and Coordination Agency, 2013).

277 Development Initatives, *Global Humanitarian Assistance Report 2015* (Bristol, Development Initiatives, 2015).

278 Imogen Mathers, "Refugee shelter re-designed" in *SciDevNet*, 18 August 2015.

279 WHS Middle East and North Africa, *Stakeholder Analysis* (2015).

280 UNHCR, "Resolving Protracted Displacement: A Contribution to the WHS", paper prepared for the WHS (2015).

281 UNICEF, *Under Siege: The devastating Impact on Children of Three Years of Conflict in Syria* (New York, United Nations, 2013).

282 UNDP and UNHCR, *Regional Strategic Overview. Regional Refugee and Resilience Plan 2015-2016: In Response to the Syria Crisis* (United Nations, 2014).

283 Milan Thomas and Nicholas Burnett, *"Exclusion from Education: The Economic Cost of Out of School Children in 20 Countries: Results for Development"* (Educate a Child and Results for Development, 2013).

284 WHS Europe and Others, *Co-Chairs' Summary* (2015).

285 Executive Committee of the High Commissioner's Programme, *Solution Strategies* (Geneva, UNHCR, 2015).

286 UNHCR, "Resolving Protracted Displacement: A Contribution to the WHS", paper prepared for the WHS (2015).

287 Alexander Betts, Louise Bloom and Nina Weaver, *Refugee Innovation: Humanitarian Innovation that Starts with Communities* (Oxford, Humanitarian Innovation Project, 2015).

Giving Cash Provides the Best Value

Owen Barder

In the following viewpoint, Owen Barder recommends providing refugees and victims of disasters with cash rather than food and other supplies. He suggests that the dissemination of cash would be less wasteful and would actually be more beneficial to both the people in need and to local economies. Owen Barder is with the Center for Global Development, a US nonprofit focused on international development.

As you read, consider the following questions:

1. How much of the money the US spent on food aid went to American contractors instead of the end recipients?
2. How does money given to refugees affect the local economy?
3. What are the risks in giving cash instead of food to refugees?

The tragic reality faced by millions of people fleeing Syrian conflict were driven home this week as we were confronted with images three-year-old Aylan Kurdi, who drowned when the boat carrying his family sank. The British public has shown again their instinct for humanity, demanding that we do more to help refugees fleeing conflict in Syria and elsewhere. As politicians try to catch up with the public mood, we should also be asking ourselves another question: how can we do more to help the millions of other refugees that do not attempt the perilous journey to safety on our shores?

Britain is already among the most generous donors to humanitarian crises. Our largest ever response – £800m to help Syrian refugees – has helped to ensure their survival through four bitter winters. Sadly, there is no end in sight to the conflict. This crisis highlights the changing nature of humanitarian emergencies, and strongly suggests that our response to these crises must change, too.

More people are in need and for longer. More than 52m people – about as many people as the population of England - are either internally displaced or living as refugees around the world. Some will be refugees for more than a decade. Kenya's dust-blown Dadaab camp has been in operation for well over two decades. Many of the 400,000 Somalis living there have never called anywhere else home.

Increasingly, though, camps are not where refugees end up. The vast majority of the millions of Syrians who have fled to neighbouring Lebanon, Turkey, and Jordan live among local populations. While some receive cash, most depend on aid supplies or vouchers for specific items. Often treated as pariahs, many of them literally fled with only what they could carry, and know that it may be many years before they can safely return home. That's one reason some keep moving; it also explains why in 2012, about four fifths of humanitarian assistance from OECD countries – a club of the world's richest economies – went to countries that are long-term recipients rather than short-term disasters.

There may be a better way to help the displaced millions facing years of poverty and insecurity: give them cash.

Consider Afghanistan, a country that Britain has been supporting for years. Traditionally, a widow in Herat, say, might receive an aid package, delivered by truck from far away, after a foreign aid agency determined what she and her children needed.

By giving her a modest cash transfer instead, she can decide what her family needs most and can be bought locally.

In this scenario, cash would be more effective and more transparent. It might also be less wasteful. International food aid, for example, is often sourced from donor countries and transported to the affected region. From 2003-2012, more than half of the $17.9bn the US spent on food aid went to American contractors. When aid is provided as supplies, part of it inevitably ends up in the pockets of foreign suppliers or middlemen. True, in the first days after a natural disaster, when there is no access to local supplies, shipments of food and medical supplies may still be vital. And some urgent problems, like treating severe malnourishment with therapeutic feeding, may require the special skills of humanitarian agencies. But what about later on?

In the Philippines, a week after Typhoon Haiyan destroyed much of Tacloban, aid agencies' noble intentions didn't always match the need. In some places, agencies provided a surfeit of cooking utensils – but no food to put in them. When road routes re-opened, tankers brought water from other parts of the Philippines– but no generators for a city without power. Instead, people charged their mobile phones from the batteries of army trucks guarding the water deliveries. At that point, could cash have more efficiently matched the supply of local markets to the demand of survivors?

Cash might also help jump-start local economies. In a trial in Lebanon, Syrian refugees were given US$100 on ATM cards: every $1 spent generated more than $2 in economic activity. In a humanitarian crisis, private sector delivery mechanisms might respond better to changing needs.

There are risks as well as opportunities from using cash. For a start, cash may be dangerous to carry for aid workers and beneficiaries. Some intriguing new options include giving out biometric ID cards that double as debit cards, or sending payments via mobile phone (as in the Kenyan M-Pesa system).

Another concern is that recipients could squander the cash they are given, or spend it on drugs or alcohol. In fact, research shows people in crisis tend to act very responsibly. Like any of us, the vast majority just want to keep their families healthy, safe and educated.

The Asian tsunami in 2004 was a wake-up call for aid agencies. Humanitarian assistance is now more coordinated, responsive and effective. It is right that Britain and other rich countries continue to help. But the global humanitarian system needs to keep pace with growing need and louder calls for greater effectiveness, transparency and accountability.

These are controversial ideas that challenge traditional aid. But as the opportunities to give people in need cash grow in number and go down in price, and as evidence grows that local markets often do respond quickly, this is a debate that we need to have. I have the privilege of chairing a panel of experts convened by the Department for International Development, the UK's aid agency, which will report on September 14th on whether, and to what extent, cash should be given instead of, or in addition to, traditional aid-in-kind.

Let's be clear: small cash payments to refugees are unlikely to deter those who want to head for Europe. But giving people cash may go some way to restoring choice and dignity for the millions more who don't, making our stretched resources stretch a little further in this time of urgent, tragic need.

Periodical and Internet Sources Bibliography

The following articles have been selected to supplement the diverse views presented in this chapter.

Dany Bahar, "How economics could solve the refugee crisis," Brookings Institution, June 16, 2016. https://www.brookings.edu/blog/future-development/2016/06/16/how-economics-could-solve-the-refugee-crisis/

Suzanne Bearne, "The global tech community tackles the refugee crisis," The Guardian, February 19, 2016. https://www.theguardian.com/media-network/2016/feb/19/global-tech-community-tackles-refugee-crisis-berlin

Pauline Bock, "The 12 startups using tech to tackle Europe's refugee crisis," Wired, September 29, 2016. http://www.wired.co.uk/article/tech-startups-refugee-crisis

Edward Dark, "How to solve the Syrian crisis," The Guardian, November 13, 2014, https://www.theguardian.com/commentisfree/2014/nov/13/solve-syrian-crisis-assad-jihadist

Jake Horowitz, "There's a Solution to the Refugee Crisis, But No One Is Talking About It," World.Mic, January 24, 2016. https://mic.com/articles/133309/there-s-a-solution-to-the-refugee-crisis-but-no-one-is-talking-about-it#.wULOXS5SN

Annie Epstein, "Can Technology Solve the Refugee Crisis?" Free Enterprise, September 21, 2016. https://www.freeenterprise.com/technology-and-the-refugee-crisis/

David Miliband, "Refugees don't waste the financial aid we send them – so we need to stop worrying that they do," Independent, 2015. http://www.independent.co.uk/voices/comment/refugees-dont-waste-the-financial-aid-we-send-them-so-we-need-to-stop-thinking-that-they-do-9760920.html

Yasmin Nouh, "6 Organizations Helping Syrian Refugees That You Might Not Have Heard Of," The Huffington Post, December 15, 2016. http://www.huffingtonpost.com/yasmin-nouh/syrian-refugee-relief-organizations_b_8142492.html

Amber Phillips, "Here's how much the United States spends on refugees," The Washington Post, November 30, 2015. https://www.washingtonpost.com/news/the-fix/wp/2015/11/30/heres-how-much-the-united-states-spends-on-refugees/

UNHCR, "6 steps towards solving the refugee situation in Europe," The UN Refugee Agency, March 4, 2016. http://www.unhcr.org/en-us/news/press/2016/3/56d957db9/unhcr-6-steps-towards-solving-refugee-situation-europe.html

Rob Williams, "Syrian refugees will cost ten times more to care for in Europe than in neighboring countries," Independent, March 13, 2016. http://www.independent.co.uk/voices/syrian-refugees-will-cost-ten-times-more-to-care-for-in-europe-than-in-neighboring-countries-a6928676.html

For Further Discussion

Chapter 1

1. What are the differences between legal immigrants, illegal immigrants, and refugees? Why is it sometimes difficult to make clear distinctions?

2. Should people be treated differently depending on whether they are immigrants or refugees? Should their age or sex make a difference in treatment? What about their country of origin or their religion? Provide reasoning for your answers.

Chapter 2

1. What are some ways allowing immigration can benefit a country? Consider the economy, the old-age dependency ratio, and society. What are some ways allowing immigration can create challenges for a country? Consider the economy, unemployment, and social stresses. How does the answer vary for different countries?

2. Marjorie Cohn claims that the US has a responsibility to help Middle Eastern refugees, because the United States helped create the crisis. David Hollenbach says that Christians should help refugees. Do certain groups have a greater responsibility to provide aid to refugees? Why or why not? Is there a limit to the type or extent of aid that should be provided? For example, should a country allow immigration, or is it enough to provide financial support?

Chapter 3

1. What are some of the challenges to integrating immigrants into society? Are there times when immigrants should not be integrated? Why or why not?

2. Why are refugees often not allowed to work? What are the benefits and disadvantages to this policy?

Chapter 4

1. Some countries have been more welcoming to immigrants than others. How do economic and social factors already existing in a country tend to affect that country's response to new immigrants?
2. Elizabeth Collett suggests that the EU-Turkey agreement could fail because it does not meet current laws. Why is it so difficult to find a solution that is legal? Is it more important to follow current legal procedures or to implement a solution quickly even if it skirts the law? What are the advantages and disadvantages to each possibility?

Chapter 5

1. Compare the International Labour Organization's recommendations for Lebanon and for Egypt in Viewpoint 1. How are the recommendations different, and why?
2. Some experts say that the refugee crisis is best met by integrating refugees into their host countries as permanent citizens. Others say the crisis should be met by giving refugees temporary shelter until they can be returned to their home country. What would have to happen for the latter solution to succeed? Could both solutions be implemented simultaneously? What seems most likely to work in the long term?

Organizations to Contact

The editors have compiled the following list of organizations concerned with the issues debated in this book. The descriptions are derived from materials provided by the organizations. All have publications or information available for interested readers. The list was compiled on the date of publication of the present volume; the information provided here may change. Be aware that many organizations take several weeks or longer to respond to inquiries, so allow as much time as possible.

Aid and International Development Forum
3rd Floor, Two America Square, London EC3N 2LU,
United Kingdom
+44 207-871-0188
website: http://www.aidforum.org/

The Aid and International Development Forum (AIDF) specializes in disaster relief, use of mobile technologies, food security, and water security. The group aims to coordinate across regions and between government agencies, nongovernmental agencies, and the private sector. Leaders in humanitarian and developmental practices share their views at worldwide events.

Amnesty International
Calle Luz Saviñon 519 Colonia del Valle, Benito Juarez
03100 Ciudad de Mexico , Mexico
+44-20-74135500
email: contactus@amnesty.org
website: http://https://www.amnesty.org/en/

Amnesty International is an international nongovernmental organization focused on human rights. The organization's interests range from torture and the death penalty to free speech. More than 7 million people in over 150 countries and territories are members.

The Brookings Institution

1775 Massachusetts Ave., NW, Washington, DC 20036
202-797-6000
email: communications@brookings.edu
website: http://https://www.brookings.edu/

The Brookings Institution is a nonprofit public policy organization. Its mission is to conduct in-depth research that leads to new ideas for solving the problems facing society at the local, national and global level.

Center for Global Development

2055 L Street NW, Fifth Floor, Washington DC 20036, USA
(202) 416-4000
email: frilling@cgdev.org
website: http://https://www.cgdev.org/

The Center for Global Development is a US nonprofit focused on international development. Their goal is to reduce global poverty and inequality by turning research and policy analysis into action. They have a newsletter aimed at educators and students.

Friends of Europe

Rue de la Science 4, 1040, Bruxelles, Belgium
Phone: +32 2-893-98-19
email: info@friendsofeurope.org
website: http://http://www.friendsofeurope.org/

Friends of Europe is a think tank focused on creating positive change in Europe through the exchange of innovative ideas. It sponsors debates and publishes reports on politics in Europe. Covered topics include Europe's social problems, the global financial crisis, and communications shortcomings.

The German Marshall Fund
1744 R St NW, Washington, DC 20009, USA
202-683-2648
email: kglover@gmfus.org
website: http://www.gmfus.org/

The German Marshall Fund (GMF) is a nonpartisan American public policy think tank. It contributes research and analysis on international issues and is dedicated to promoting cooperation between North America and Europe. A particular focus is the Balkans and the Black Sea regions.

The Heritage Foundation
214 Massachusetts Ave NE , Washington DC 20002-4999, USA
202-546-4400
email: info@heritage.org
website: http://http://www.heritage.org/

The Heritage Foundation is a conservative research center. Its goal is to effectively communicate conservative policy research to Congress and the American people. Issues include health care reform, immigration, and terrorism.

International Labour Organization
4 route des Morillons, CH-1211, Genève 22, Switzerland
+41 (0) 22-799-6111
email: ilo@ilo.org
website: http://www.ilo.org/

The International Labour Organization is a United Nations agency. The ILO works with governments, employers, and workers representatives to promote decent work for all women and men. Representatives of 187 countries are involved in setting labor standards and developing policies and programs.

Mercy Corps
45 SW Ankeny St., Portland, OR 97204, USA
800-292-3355
email: https://www.mercycorps.org/contact
website: http://www.mercycorps.org/

Mercy Corps is a global agency that provides humanitarian and development assistance around the world. The agency's goal is to alleviate suffering, poverty, and oppression, and to help create more secure, productive, and just communities.

Migration Policy Institute
1400 16th Street NW, Suite 300, Washington, DC 20036, USA
202-266-1940
email: Info@MigrationPolicy.org
website: http://www.migrationpolicy.org/

The Migration Policy Institute (MPI) is a nonpartisan, nonprofit think tank based in Washington DC. MPI provides analysis and evaluation of migration and refugee policies. Its guiding philosophy is that international migration needs active and intelligent management. MPI publishes an online journal.

Bibliography of Books

Maurizio Albahari, *Crimes of Peace: Mediterranean Migrations at the Word's Deadliest Border*. Philadelphia, PA: University of Pennsylvania, 2015.

Mark Bixler, *The Lost Boys of Sudan: An American Story of the Refugee Experience*. Athens, GA: University of Georgia Press, 2006.

Peter Morton Coan, *Toward A Better Life: America's New Immigrants in Their Own Words from Ellis Island to the Present*. Amherst, NY: Prometheus Books, 2011.

Diego Cupolo, *Seven Syrians: War Accounts from Syrian Refugees*. New York, NY: 8th House Publishing, 2013.

Edwidge Danticat, *Brother, I'm Dying*. New York, NY: Random House, 2007.

Elena Fiddian-Qasmiyeh, Gil Loescher, Katy Long, and Nando Sigona, eds., *The Oxford Handbook of Refugee and Forced Migration Studies*. Oxford, United Kingdom: Oxford University, 2014.

Peter Gatrell, *The Making of The Modern Refugee*. Oxford, United Kingdom: Oxford University Press, 2013.

Jeremy Harding, *Border Vigils: Keeping Migrants Out of the Rich World*. London, United Kingdom and New York, NY: Verso, 2012.

Reece Jones, *Violent Borders: Refugees and the Right to Move*. London, United Kingdom and New York, NY: Verso, 2016.

Patrick Kingsley, *The New Odyssey: The Story of Europe's Refugee Crisis*. Norwich, UK: Guardian Faber Publishing, 2016.

Gulwali Passarlay, *The Lightless Sky: My Journey to Safety as a Child Refugee*. London, United Kingdom: Atlantic Books, 2016.

Ben Rawlence, *City of Thorns: Nine Lives in the World's Largest Refugee Camp*. London, United Kingdom: Picador, 2017.

Margaret Regan, *The Death of Josseline: Immigration Stories from the Arizona Borderlands*. Boston, MA: Beacon Press, 2010.

Luis Alberto Urrea, *The Devil's Highway: A True Story*. New York, NY: Back Bay Books, 2005.

Index